Coach Tex Winter
Triangle
Basketball

by
Ann Parr

Copyright 2006 by Ann Parr
Library of Congress Number 2006927221
ISBN: 978-1-933803-10-4
Published
by
NDX Press
Nashville, TN

Art credits:

Ann Parr: Pages 107, 115, 129, 141, 147.

Barry Elz: Front cover.

Bill Smith: Pages 9, 78, 93, 94, 95, 99, 101, 102, 104, 105, 108,
109, 111, 113, 117, 119, 120, 123, 124, 125, 126.

Blog for Veterans: Page 42.

Compton College Athletic Department: Pages 27, 29.

Daniel Gluskoter: Back cover, pages 9, 132.

David Markweise: Back cover.

Gene Schramka: Page 56.

Hayden Abbott: Page 141.

Hugh Morton: Page 112

Huntington Park High School, Javier Vazquez: Pages 9, 26.

Kansas Sports Hall of Fame: Pages 8, 10, 34, 48, 52, 61, 62,
90, 128, 144.

Kansas State University Special Collections: Pages 7, 9, 47,
53, 57, 60, 65, 66, 89, 127.

Kansas State University Sports Information: Pages 9, 50,
69, 71, 142, 143.

Ken Smith: Page 37.

Long Beach State University: Pages 9, 82, 85.

Louisiana State University: Pages 9, 86.

Loyola University: Page 74

Marquette University: Pages 9, 54, 55.

Naval Historical Center: Page 40-image #NH97484; page
43-image #80-G-14548.

NBA Photo Archives: Pages 96, 129, 131, 134, 137, 139, 140,
145, 146.

Northwestern University: Pages 9, 81.

Robyn Zurfluh: Page 34.

Texas Tech University Special Collections: Pages 19, 20.

Tex Winter: Back cover, pages 9, 12, 15, 16, 17, 18, 22, 24, 25,
30, 32, 35, 36, 38, 44, 49, 51, 67, 68, 70, 77, 88, 144.

University of North Carolina: Page 91.

University of Washington: Pages 9, 73.

Acknowledgements

This book is the result of a team effort—a concept Tex advocates and has lived all his life. Many generous and interested players, family, and friends have contributed to the collection of data that forms this story of Tex's life.

I am grateful:

To former players who completed surveys about their experiences with Tex as teacher and coach and permitted me to use their words.

To family members, friends, and colleagues who granted interviews and gave time to track down photographs.

To college and university athletic and special collection departments for photograph and name searches.

To Barry Elz for use of the front cover photograph.

To Kent Fellers and his design team at Arrow Printing Company, especially Liz Knaus for her client-sensitive creative work.

To Tex for the privilege of working with his life story, witnessing its flow uphill and downhill, never losing its focus on his life's work as teacher and coach.

To my husband, Jack Parr, for knowing how to undo my ill-fitting sports descriptions, when to say a word of encouragement, and where to remain during the entire production of this book—at my right side.

Ann Parr

Foreword

Tex Winter began his coaching career in the fall of 1947 as assistant coach at Kansas State University and continues through this season, 2005–06 as assistant coach and consultant with the Los Angeles Lakers. He has stayed in the field, teaching and coaching, nearly sixty consecutive seasons, except for the 2004–05 season when he followed through on his threat to retire. The retirement lasted one season.

This book highlights Tex's background, values and character; how he found his love for sports, followed it, and thrived. It follows the development of his major contribution to the game of basketball—the Triple Post Offense, often called the Triangle Offense. It provides background for the Triangle's evolution, and it underlines the sometimes rocky and painful road to the legacy he leaves. As his friend Pete Newell says, "He changed the game of basketball and gave a name to a particular pattern of offense."

Most of all, this book shows how Tex Winter became the teacher and coach that he, as a young teen, defined as his life's work.

Coach Tex Winter:
Triangle Basketball

CONTENTS

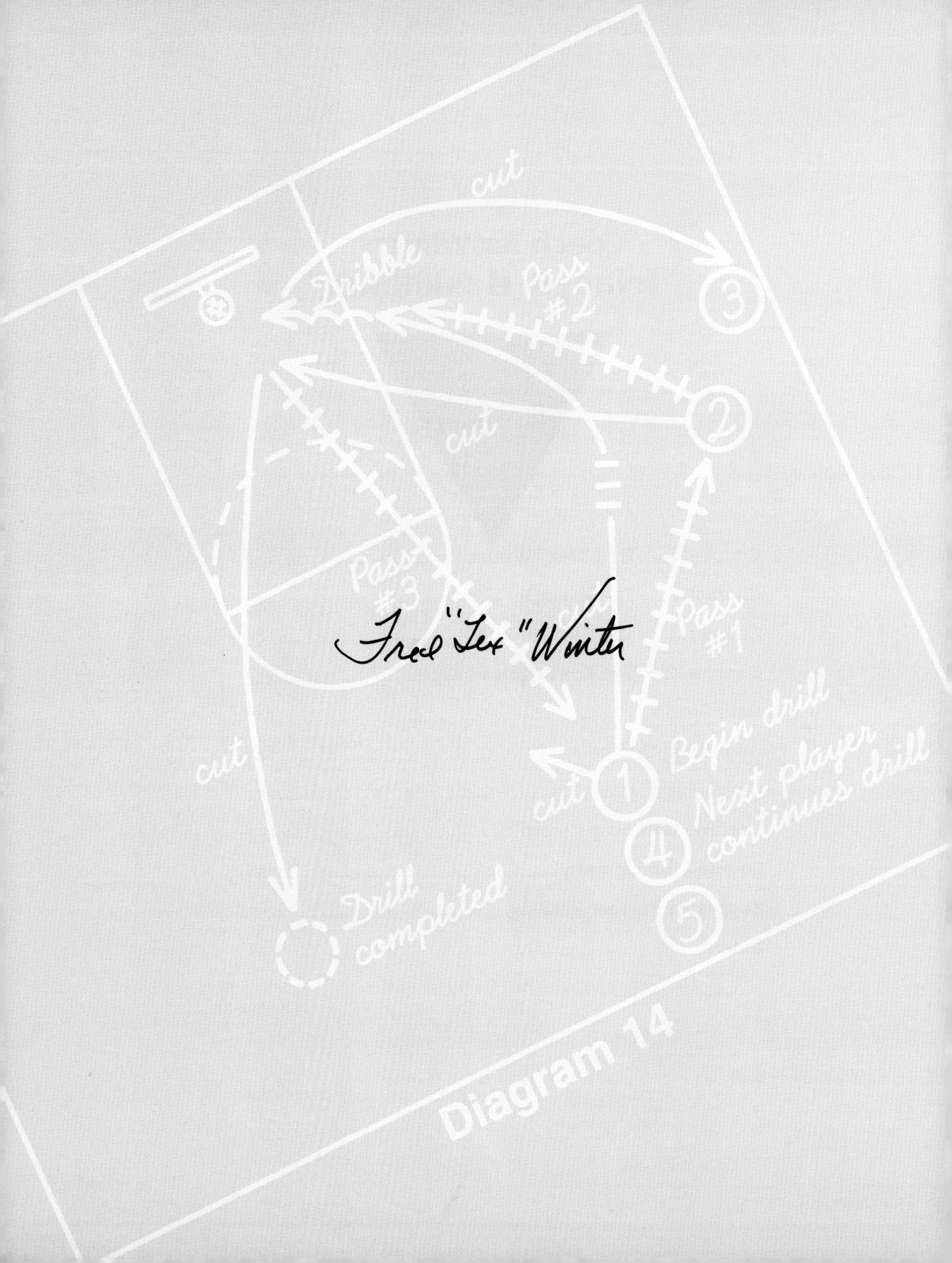

Fred "Tex" Winter

Diagram 14

Offensive Build-Up Drills

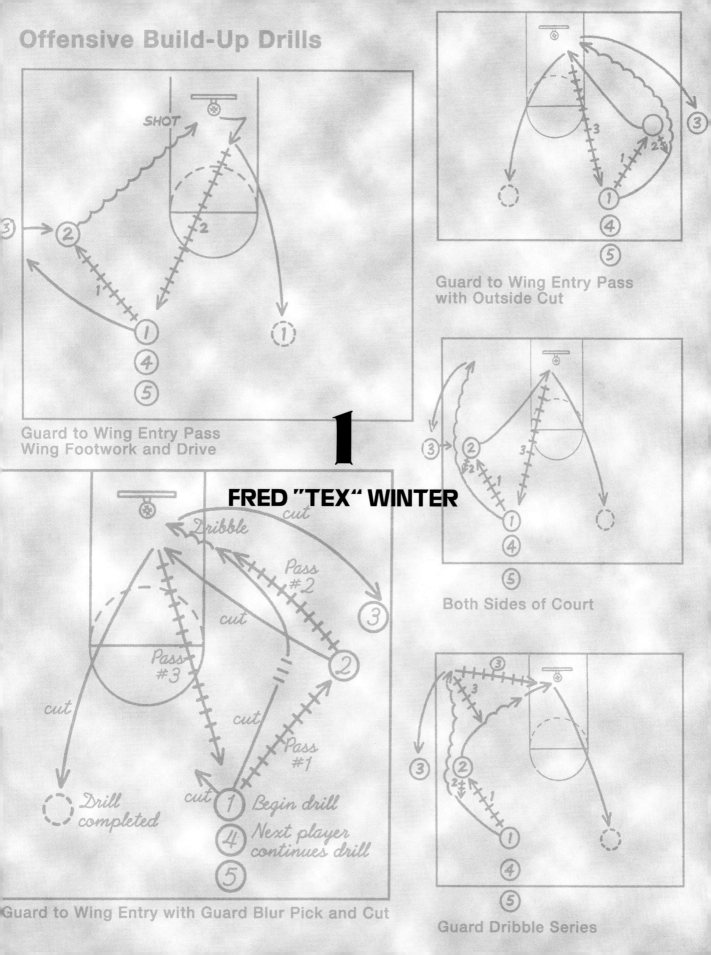

Guard to Wing Entry Pass
Wing Footwork and Drive

Guard to Wing Entry Pass
with Outside Cut

Both Sides of Court

Guard to Wing Entry with Guard Blur Pick and Cut

Guard Dribble Series

FRED "TEX" WINTER

1

State of Ka
Sports Hall of
TEX WIN
Inducted Jul

COACH WINTER

From his lookout on the Huntington Park California High School bleachers, Fred Winter's eyes followed the cagers up and down the basketball court. "Come on. Rotate," Coach Jimmy Needles called to his 1937 Loyola University line-up. "You're a team. Somebody will be there, so pass the ball quick."

Lines crisscrossed every which way on Fred's clipboard pages, tracing the movement of the basketball, an X identifying each offensive player and an O for each defensive player. "When I call reverse action," Coach Needles continued, "stay spaced, spread out across the floor, and move the ball."

Fred traced the Xs as they spun into triangles according to Coach Needles's instructions. More images of ways to move the ball in and out of the triangle shape popped into Fred's head in the middle of classes during the day and sneaked into his dreams at night. He recorded them on clipboard pages, piled high, carefully filed away. Even though Fred had two more years of high school, he took a deep breath, grabbed the biggest marker he could find, and poster-printed across the page, "I'm going to be a coach."

Coach Jimmy Needles, Loyola University of Los Angeles.

> The one common denominator to all success and happiness is other people.

The Loyola University of Los Angeles basketball team, coached by Jimmy Needles, practiced in our Huntington Park High School gymnasium every evening after school. I was kind of a "ball-shagger" for the team. The Los Angeles earthquake of 1933 destroyed many buildings, and our gym had been rebuilt. I thought Needles would let me stay if I made myself useful. His "reverse action" type of offense was the first triangle positioning I had ever seen. I wrote down every one of those plays.

cut

Dribble

Pass #2

cut

cut

Pass #3

cut

Pass #1

cut

1) Begin drill

4) Next player continues drill

5)

Fred, clipboard in hand, stayed every evening after his own basketball practices to watch the Loyola team. He listed plays called, shots attempted, and baskets made under pre-labeled headings in orderly columns. "Lookin' good," Coach Needles encouraged his team. "Keep it movin.' No standing around. I want to see you positioned around the court and moving the ball. Stay spaced and reverse the ball with sharply-aimed pin-point passes."

Fred noticed how Needles's triangle-shaped plans outwitted the defense players time after time. He took more notes. Keep the basketball moving. Pass instead of dribble. All players move with purpose. Keep the court spaced, and read the defense.

Each page included a checklist of warm-up exercises and small group drills and code words for plays that sent Fred's mind soaring. He would teach his players about the game. He would insist that they give their best. He would have his own world-class team. ▲ (Please read large red triangle, page 10.)

Fred "Tex" first shot baskets in this hoop on his family's farm.

Tex says

The only basketball I had known until Huntington Park was shooting at a peach basket on our barn or in a vacant lot in Lubbock with friends—you know, the kind of play where you count to see how many baskets you make.

Tex says

E. C. Neander, my coach for the "D" and "C" teams, and Pop Squire, my next coach for the "B" team, told me I had exceptional ability. You're not very big, they said, but maybe you'll grow. I learned about making a contribution. I guess it paid off, because if you don't make a contribution as a player or a coach, you're not going to be around very long. I learned the importance of surrounding yourself with good people.

Fred and his family had moved from Lubbock, Texas to Huntington Park, California, a suburb of Los Angeles. All the Los Angeles schools ranked athletes according to height, weight, and age. Fred tried out for basketball right away. At five-foot-six, 106 pounds, Fred made the D team and was elected captain. For the spring semester, Fred wanted to join the track team. But when he went for his school physical exam, the doctor said, "You can't run distances." ▲ *(Please read large black triangle, page 12.)*

Fred's shoulders drooped, and he let out a big sigh. Although he wasn't surprised to learn that his heart muscle measured larger from hard workouts, he still wanted to be part of a team. If he didn't run distances, he would try something else. He high-jumped, long-jumped, and ran hurdles. He won his first athletic letter.

As a junior, he picked up a pole. He soon became one of the top vaulters in the city. Although a difficult and somewhat risky sport, Fred showed the bravery and desire to master it.

Tex continued to play basketball. He joined the C team his junior year and the B team his senior year. Both teams elected him captain. Fred's teammates liked his quickness on the floor and the way he could follow each player's position. They also noticed the accent in his speech, his Texas drawl. They started calling him Tex, a nickname Fred wished had stayed in Texas. But he was stuck with it for life.

"You've got the knack for this," basketball Coaches Neander and Squire told him.

Fred's chest puffed out a little farther as he pictured himself contributing to a great team, hustling around the defense, finding and making the best shots. He remained after practice each evening, inventing plays with those who would stay and scrimmage with him.

Fred's plan became clearer. Pay attention to what worked for his coaches, and remember their encouragement of him. Teach fundamental moves and strategies as Coach Needles did with his Loyola team. Give players encouraging but honest feedback as Coaches Neanders and Squire did. Analyze why some ideas worked better than others.

Tex would build on the combination of others' ideas blended with his own. He would become a great teacher and a great coach. ▲ *(Please read large orange triangle, page 12.)*

I was the baby of the family by fifteen minutes. My mother named me Morice Fredrick, and my twin sister, Mona Francis. We were born February 25, 1922.

Mother was hysterical. She had Mona first, and she really struggled. The doctor said, "Wait a minute, we've got another one."

She said, "No, no, no, no. I don't want it. Put it back."

The doctor said, "Well, I'll take it."

She said, "Well, you can have it."

For a long time, that doctor claimed me. He teased my mother and said, "That's my boy."

But she said, "No, we're a family. I've got to keep Fred with me."

"We both lived on Fourth Street in Lubbock. The Junior High School was on Tenth or Eleventh. We would run home as fast as we could—not to hurry, but for exercise. Freddie would say, "Come on and have some oats." His mom would feed us oatmeal. Fred's motto might be, 'Do your best with what you have.' It fits the way he was raised."

Maurice L. Tinsley

Maurice Tinsley
Fred "Tex's" life-long friend

While I lived in Lubbock, a black kid named Rufus and I were the best marble players on the south side of Lubbock. That was my first experience with a black. I really loved the guy. He was a better marble player than I was, and I was pretty good. In Lubbock, at 7 or 8 o'clock in the evening, depending on when it turned dark, the sirens would go off. Rufus would grab his marbles and head out. He didn't say "bye" or anything. I never understood it. I started asking around, "What's the siren all about? Some storm or something?"

"No, no. That's a curfew for the blacks to get on their side of the tracks."

I've often wondered what happened to Rufus. I haven't seen him since I left Lubbock. I didn't even know his last name.

Fred "Tex," his mother, and his sons visit the house near Wellington, Texas where Tex lived as a child.

After moving to Lubbock, Fred "Tex" met a lifetime "best friend," Maurice Tinsley. Tex is on the right.

When Fred was born, he and his family lived in a small house on the Winter family farm near Wellington, Texas. Fred's father helped with farming, but preferred to make a living as a mechanic.▲

The family moved to Lubbock when Fred was seven. His dad became the master mechanic at a Chevrolet dealership. Mr. Winter made good money at his new job, Fred hung out with friends up and down the street, and the family enjoyed their larger home in town. But the Winters' new life lasted only a short time.▲

Back row: Mrs. Winter (Theo); Tex's older sister Elizabeth; Mr. Winter (Marion Ernest). Front row: Tex's twin sister Mona Francis; Tex's older brother Marion Ernest, Jr.; Tex, (Morice Fredrick).

Tex says

Dad loved to fish and was off on a deep-sea fishing expedition with some buddies. But I knew something had gone wrong a few days later when my mother gripped the telephone. "Mr. Winter was finned by a manta ray," the voice said. "Not far off the Gulf of Mexico. It's pretty bad."

An infection from a deep gash in his right leg grew steadily worse. The doctors wanted to remove the infected section, which meant an amputation at the hip. "Absolutely not," Dad said.

Tex's father, Marion Ernest Winter.

In December 1932 when Fred was ten, a crowd of family and friends had gathered in the Wellington Presbyterian Church. Usually Texans getting together meant a party with hay bales and music and square dancing, but when Fred looked at people's eyes, they glanced away. Conversations turned to whispers. This was no party. It was a funeral for Fred's father.

Dad had died of a bad infection in his leg, and no one seemed to know what to do. ▲ The Winter family, already suffering the effects of the Great Depression, had lost their breadwinner. They faced an unwelcome future.

After the funeral, nothing seemed real, yet time passed. Ernest, Fred's thirteen-year-old brother, started taking charge of Fred. With their mother gone all day working at a women's clothing store, Fred's sixteen-year-old sister, Elizabeth, began directing Fred's twin sister, Mona. Fred and Mona tried to do what both Ernest and Elizabeth told them. Without Dad, they had to learn how to be a family all over again.

"After our dad died, Fred would let me tell him what to do, and he would do it. He was a very helpful little kid. I just remember that he was always the one that sat back and let everybody else take the stage. He never tried to put himself forward."

Elizabeth Winter Green

Elizabeth Winter Green,
Fred "Tex's" older sister

Fred "Tex," right, and his older brother Ernest in 1932.

Tex says

After collecting all those boxes for the bakery, I became known as the "Box Boy." I still love boxes. I gather them all the time. Once in a while the equipment guys will save a couple of the better ones for me. And of course, I have Michael Jordan's Nike shoe boxes that I store under my desk. They still kid me to this day. "Tex, we saved you a good box!"

A scene from downtown Lubbock, Texas, 1928.

Each week, Ernest handed Fred a stack of advertising flyers to distribute around the neighborhood. The store owner paid them a penny for each one delivered.

Next they searched alleys, looking for stray cardboard boxes. The local baker gave them day-old bread in exchange for the boxes used to pack baked goods for delivery. ▲ Fred also sold Sunday newspapers in front of Pinson's Drug Store where he worked as a part-time soda jerk.

Occasionally Fred and Ernest walked to the grain bins down the road to get a bucket of wheat. Mrs. Winter would cook the wheat at night for two or three hours. They ate it for breakfast with condensed milk, one can of milk diluted with four cans of water. The family did not have extras, but they had each other.

Central Wood School, Lubbock, Texas, where Fred "Tex" attended junior high.

A fellow teammate may be faster than you; he may be a better shot or a more clever passer; may be a better defensive player; and he might be taller and heavier—but he should not be superior in team spirit, fight, determination, ambition, and character.

Fred joined the Lubbock Junior High School track team. The 1935 seventh-grade county spring meet was ready to begin. "Freddie Winter to lane nine," the announcer shouted.

Fred stuck his toe to the starting line.

Earlier, Ernest had won the ninth-grade 880-yard race. Poised like a watchdog, he kept a straight-ahead gaze on the track. "Go get 'em, Freck," Ernest said, using his nickname for Fred.

Fred charged out of the starting line. He caught Ernest's eye as he came around the first lap, then the second. Fred was running the 880–yard event only because Ernest had said he'd beat Fred up if he didn't run. Fred gasped what felt like his last breath and slid into the pack next to last.

"Come on Freck. Come on. Turn it on," Ernest shouted as he moved to the inside curb.

"I'm going to drop out," Fred wheezed back.

"You do, and you'll answer to me."

Fred found a second wind and passed runners down the backstretch. He continued around the last turn and into the straight-away. He hit the tape just ahead of the first runner and fell flat on his face in the cinder track. He had beaten Ernest's best time by two-tenths of a second and won his first-ever athletic event.

Ernest jumped over the barrier to scrape Fred off the track. "Proud of you, man," he yelled as he thumped him on the back, his eyes wide. Fred could tell that Ernest was surprised that his little brother had shattered his own record. Ernest punched Fred in the shoulder and grinned. "Well, you never would have done it without me." Fred believed him.

As a newspaper reporter's camera flashed in Fred's face, he stumbled around and blinked. He had not expected to do so well. Winning the race caught him up short and showered him with recognition he wasn't sure how to handle. He couldn't figure out whether he was a star or what.

Fred raised a hand to his cheering teammates and limped off the track. His eyesight was cloudy. His lungs hurt, and his feet burned like fire. But the more his head cleared, the more he realized that pushing to win gave the team more points, and he had pushed himself. He could see that a team won when all its players did their best. He had done his best.

The Winter siblings, 1942.
Back row: Fred "Tex" and Ernest.
Front row: Mona and Elizabeth.

Wishing will never make it so, but work will fix it so that if you think you can, you will.

By the time Fred attended high school, his big sister Elizabeth had married and moved to California. "Come on out here," she urged her mother. "There are better job opportunities."

Mrs. Winter pondered the idea.

Ernest wanted to stay with his football team at Lubbock High School and did not take well to the idea of moving. Neither did Fred. "But this is where we are a family," Fred told his mother.

Mona, an easy-going sort, said California or Texas made no difference to her.

At last, Mrs. Winter made her decision. The twins, Fred and Mona, would go with her to California. Ernest would stay in Texas to play football, live at a boarding house where he would work to pay his way, and spend summers in California with the family.

Fred did not like the idea of the family being apart, but at least they would be together some of the time.

In those days—the mid 1930s—car owners in the Dust Bowl states of Texas, Oklahoma, and Kansas, hired drivers and sold seats to California. For five dollars each, Fred, his mother, and Mona piled into the back seat of the next car and headed west on Route 66.

Tex says

I am not stingy, like
some people might think,
but I will always be frugal. I
save the little soaps and
shampoo bottles from hotel rooms. I
can't waste food, and I look for the least
expensive airline tickets, even if the times
aren't just right. I lived through times when we
barely had enough, and I won't forget.

Fred "Tex," left, and brother Ernest, with their
mom, Theo.

"I had assumed the world was a
more-or-less perfect place, so it came as
a wake-up call when Mom and Dad told
me about growing up during the
Depression. I admired them for being
able to overcome those difficulties
through patience, hard work, and faith."

Brian Winter
Fred "Tex's" youngest son

24

WATERMELONS
1/2 ¢
POUND

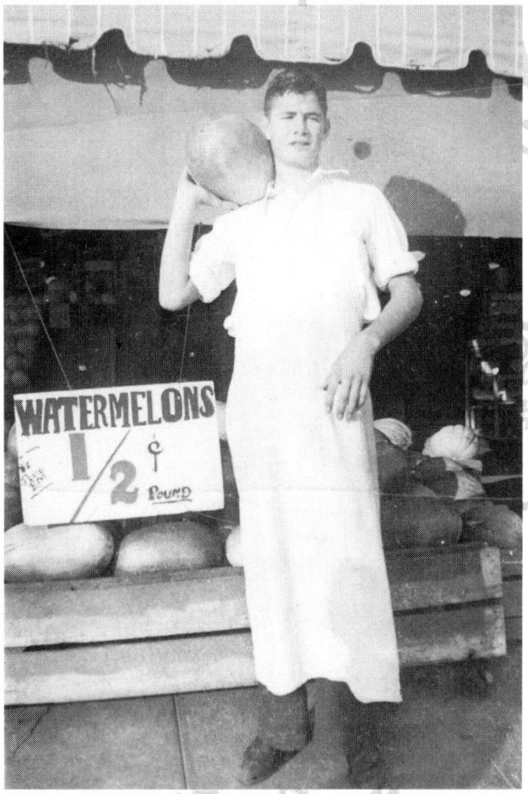

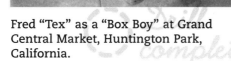

Fred "Tex" as a "Box Boy" at Grand Central Market, Huntington Park, California.

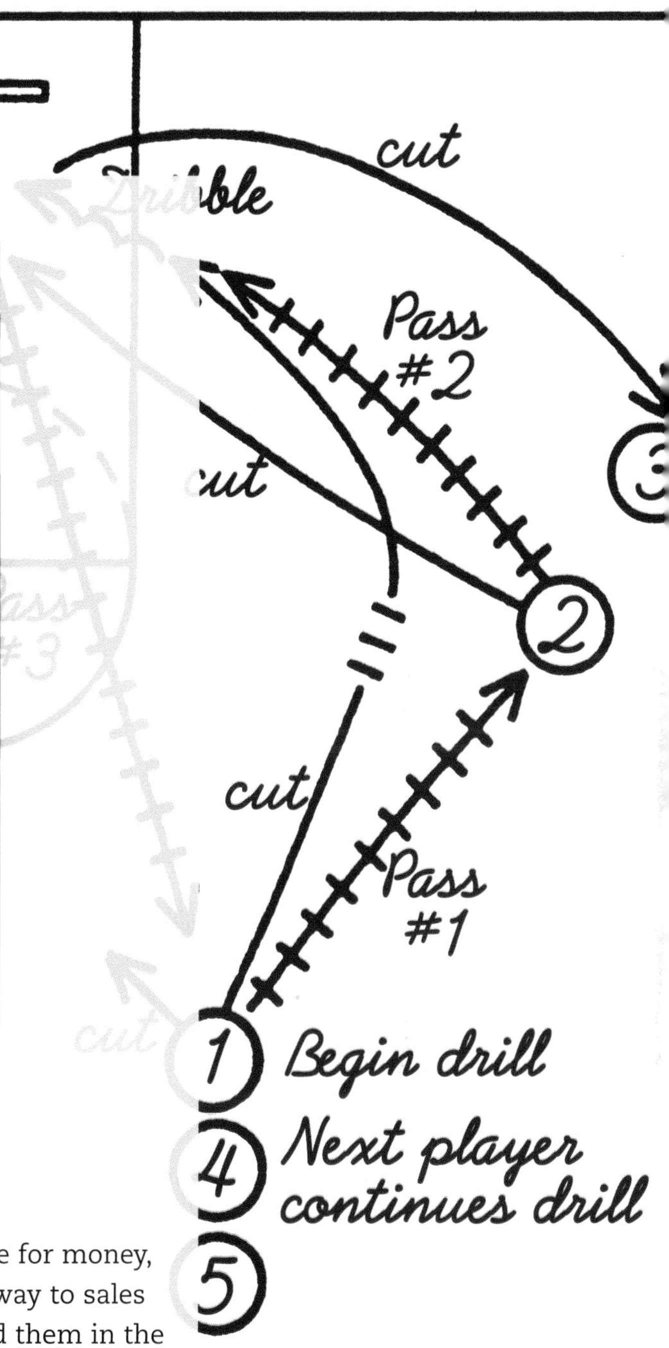

cut
Dribble
Pass
#2
cut
Pass
#3
cut
Pass
#1
cut
1 Begin drill
4 Next player continues drill
5
Drill completed

Even though Fred's family continued to struggle for money, they were a family again. Mrs. Winter worked her way to sales manager at a women's clothing store. Ernest joined them in the summers and found a job at Grand Central Market in Huntington Park and one for Fred too. Whenever customers called, "Box Boy," Fred and Ernest filled their big, white aprons with vegetables and fruits and carried them to the cars, earning a tip of a nickel or a dime. "They ought to call us Apron Boys," Fred told Ernest.

Fred pocketed his tips and took home his pay in day-old vegetables and fruits, a welcome, healthy addition to the family's meals.▲

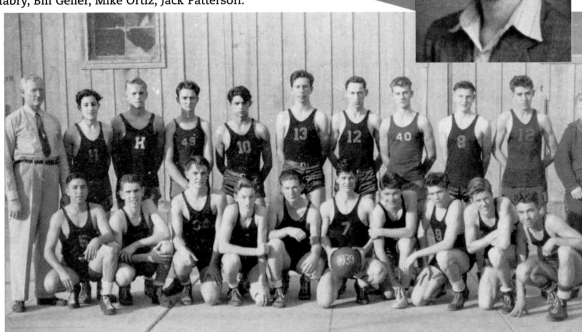

HPHS "C" Team 1938

Back row, left to right:
Bill Eccles,
Reynold Linroth,
Vernon Dyson,
Paul Mansfield,
Keith Murphy,
Carl Duncan,
Gordon Jackson.

Middle row:
Mickey Ward,
Manager; S. Ukito,
Tony Demetriou,
Ed Murphy,
Victor Allstead,
Bob Copeland,
Raymond Olson,
Kenneth Neary,
Richard Barry,
Manager.

Front row:
Coach E. C. Neander,
Joe Rosas, Fredrick Winter,
Johnny Popoff, Arthur Diaz,
Eugene Rock, Bob Dunn, Bob Binyon.

Tex says

After I graduated from high school, midterm 1940, and before I enrolled at Compton in the fall, I spent my time working, playing basketball, and pole vaulting. I built my own pit. That's when I really developed my form and increased my height.

HPHS "B" Team 1939

Standing, left to right:
Coach R. E. Squire,
Max Levine, Reynold Lindroth,
Vanon Dyson, Harold Nemser, Roy Nesbitt,
Bob Greer, Dale Mabry, Bill Geller, Mike Ortiz, Jack Patterson.

Kneeling, left to right:
Art Diaz,
Carl Bauer,
George Hachten,
Jack Winters,
Kenny Wren,
Fred Winter (#7),
Audrey Rock,
Bob Dunn,
Ed Murphy,
John Popoff.

Tex, #31, playing basketball at Compton Junior College, Huntington Park, California, against Don Cecil, #8; and Bob Howard, #5; from Long Beach Junior College.

At the end of each summer, Ernest returned to Texas where he earned All-State in football and a scholarship to Texas Tech University. Fred, now known as Tex, resumed daily basketball practices at Huntington Park High School. Eager to improve and encouraged by each coach, Tex moved from the "D" team as a sophomore, to the "C" team as a junior, and to the "B" team as a senior. He did not play the "A" team because of his size. He worked hard and became a dedicated student of the game, determined to make a college team.

Following high school, Tex enrolled at Compton Junior College in the fall of 1940 where he played basketball and pole vaulted. ▲ He had grown four inches to five-foot-eleven and weighed 140 pounds. The University of Southern California offered him a pole vaulting scholarship, but he did not qualify academically. USC's basketball coach, Sam Barry, told him to stay at Compton and improve his grades.

Tex says

I played basketball against Jackie Robinson in summer league play when I was attending Compton. One time when we were playing he said, "Shorty, I'm going to run you down." And he did.

What an athlete Jackie was. Even though he became famous for breaking the color barrier with the Brooklyn Dodgers by being the first black to play major league baseball in 1947, I think he was more outstanding at basketball and track. He was a twenty-four-foot long-jumper and played football at UCLA. He was a great, great athlete.

Good observance of training rules must come from within you, the players. It cannot in any way be forced upon you.

Tex says

With the vaulting technique I developed, I threw myself to clear the bar and landed flat on my back. On one of my vaults at Gunnison, I couldn't move my legs after I landed. They called an ambulance and took me to the hospital. They put me on a gurney with weights all around me to hold me in a certain position while waiting to examine me. While lying there, I felt a tingling, and life came back into my legs. I threw the weights off the gurney, ran out, and got on the bus to go home.

Most of the strength on this championship squad was found in the field events where the Compton Tartars won a majority of first places. The star point-getters on the jaysee squad included "Tex" Winter, pole-vault.

Tex pole vaulting at Compton Junior College, Huntington Park, California.

cut

Pass #2

Pass #1

(1) *Begin drill*

(4) *Next player continues drill*

(5)

Tex finished two years at Compton where he played basketball for Coach Tay Brown, a student of Sam Barry. A hard-nosed, no-nonsense type coach, Coach Brown taught Coach Barry's principles of "Center Opposite" offense. Tex appreciated the chance to learn Barry's offense. The Compton team could beat all but Long Beach Junior College, the team that won the state championship. In his second year, he made the All-State Junior College basketball team. ▲ Pole-vaulting at 13' 11 ¼", he set the college's record that held until fiber glass poles replaced bamboo poles. He tied for second place in the National Junior College Championships in Gunnison, Colorado. ▲

"Hey, come with us," Don Cecil and Bob Howard from Long Beach Junior College called to Tex. They were on a train headed for Oregon State University where they had basketball scholarships. Tex was on his way to San Jose State University to work with his cousin Bud Winter, a famous track coach. "We'll call Coach "Slats" Gill at Oregon State and tell him about your All-State honors at Compton," his fellow passengers said.

Tex clears a 14'4" vault in the Los Angeles Colesium into a sawdust pit using a bamboo pole. Tex high jumped, hurdled, and pole vaulted off his right foot. Therefore, carrying the pole in his left hand gave the impression that he was left-handed.

Tex says

The 1943 National NCAA Track Meet Championships were at Northwestern University's stadium in Chicago. At Oregon State, we had a half-miler who qualified, and I qualified in pole vaulting. Our coaches debated a long time about whether or not to send us because of the war. They finally decided we would go by train. It was a long trip. I won third place.

I went on and did well at the University of Southern California. I had an opportunity to be on the Olympic team. The guy who won the Olympics in 1948 was Guinn Smith. His height was 14'4", which is what I did, and I had beaten him in several meets my senior year.

The diagram labels shown: *Dribble*, *cut*, *Pass #2*, *cut*, *cut*, *Pass #1*, with circled numbers 3, 2, 1, 4, 5, and the notes *Begin drill*, *Next player continues drill*.

Tex excelled in sports at Compton, but he still did not do well in his studies. He failed some classes; his grades were bad. When he applied at Oregon State, he had to go before a board. After looking at Tex's grades, one interviewer said, "Winter, how long do you expect to get by on your looks and personality?"

The board said he could be accepted on probation into the Agronomy Department because the requirements were lower. This acceptance also granted Tex an educational deferment from military service in World War II until the end of the school year.

Tex was offered an Oregon State basketball scholarship. Joining his new friends, Bob Howard and Don Cecil, Tex worked hard to help the team and to gain a starting position, but the other players were better. He continued to notice how good each player had to be for the overall team's success.

Tex wondered if his status as a nationally-ranked pole vaulter would mean something. When basketball season ended, he approached the track coach. "What about me on your team?" he asked.

"We've got a couple of good vaulters here at Oregon State," the coach replied.

"How high?" Tex asked.

"Oh, they're thirteen-footers," the coach said.

"I did 13' 11¼" in junior college."

The coach's mouth dropped open as he grabbed the records. He didn't hesitate a second. "We'll take you," he said.

By the end of the first track meet, Tex had made a mark at Oregon State in pole vaulting. He won the Pacific Coast Conference championship and placed third in National Championships by vaulting 14' with a bamboo pole into a saw-dust pit. ▲

Nancy Bohnenkamp,
Tex's future wife, in
her WAVES uniform.

"When I first met Nancy at a dinner at their home, I was astounded to see her eat dessert first. She said she wanted to make sure she had room for it. I thought this lady had to be one of the most sophisticated people I had ever met. However, years later, when I married my wife, I found out she did the same thing."

Jerry O'Brien
Jerry O'Brien
Marquette University 1955

Before you louse it up—Think! After you've loused it up—Smile!

A couple of weeks before the spring semester ended at Oregon State, a teammate brought a message to Tex. "There's this cute little Kappa that wants to meet you."

The Kappa's name was Nancy Bohnenkamp from LeGrande, Oregon. Tex walked over to the Kappa Kappa Gamma Sorority House where she lived with her sorority sisters. She asked him about basketball. They drank sodas. They went for long walks because Tex had no money for dates. "I've signed up for the Navy pilot program," Tex told her. He had completed the required two years of college, passed the stringent physical fitness and vision tests, and qualified for the United States V-5 Navy Flight Training. "I'm going as soon as school is out."

"And I'm going to Whitman College next fall," Nancy replied.

Tex and Nancy stayed in touch while he was in the Navy and she attended Whitman.

Nancy joined the WAVES—Women Accepted as Volunteers for Emergency Service—hoping to be stationed near Tex. She was sent to Bremerton, Washington, reached only by ferryboat from Seattle. Tex was in Sanford, Florida. They had to settle for an occasional letter.

Haley Landis's Chuck Taylor All Star Converse tennis shoes, 2005.

Lucius Allen's Chuck Taylor All Star Converse basketball shoe, 1955.

Tex says

Chuck Taylor, my first commanding officer, was the developer of the famous Converse basketball shoes. My teams wore Chuck Taylor Converse shoes. The story goes that Taylor walked into the Converse Chicago sales office in the summer of 1921 complaining of sore feet. He persuaded Marquis Converse, the company founder, to make a shoe especially for basketball. In 1932, Converse added Taylor's signature to its trademark. They filled the trunk of a white Cadillac with shoes, and Taylor hit the road. Customers like me could buy them in black or white, low-cut or high tops. Today I see them in all colors, shapes, and patterns.

Tex playing basketball for the Navy with the Skyhawks while stationed at Pre-Flight School in Iowa.

Tex's first assignment was Navy V-5 Ground School at Monmouth College in Monmouth, Illinois. Unlike junior college and Oregon State, he immediately applied his studies and worked hard. He noted how qualities he had developed as an athlete—aggressiveness, desire to compete, ability to perform alone—served him well in the Navy. His quick reflexes, good balance, and keen eyesight helped too. He excelled in both the classroom and in the physical training and qualified for promotion to War Training School at Marquette University in Milwaukee, Wisconsin.

Tex's commanding officer, Chuck Taylor, assembled his group and asked, "Anyone here play basketball?" ▲

Tex answered, "Yes sir. I do."

"Bill Chandler, coach of the Marquette University team, is having tryouts. Be there."

Tex became starting guard on the team for the rest of the season while his own Navy unit moved on to Pre-Flight Training at the University of Iowa in Iowa City. Tex enjoyed being part of a basketball team again, but he lost his place with his first Navy group. Tex also pole vaulted at an indoor track meet with the

In their Navy uniforms, Texas a Cadet, left, and Ernest, Lt. Jr. Grade, right, visit their grandfather Marion Winter, 1944.

Tex says

My pilot training, intense and exciting, was really tough. It involved more studying than I had ever done in high school or college. I dug in and did pretty well. I thought I could be a good student if I applied myself, and I was.

"We're holding you over," my commanding officer said when he called me into his office.

"What? I failed?"

"Oh, no," the officer replied. "We want you to pole vault in our station's upcoming track meet."

A pattern became obvious. When my training class moved on to the next station, I was detained. The first time to play basketball. Next, to pole vault. Over and over. I could see myself as a Cadet forever, playing sports, never getting my wings.

A Stearman Yellow Peril airplane like Tex flew in the Navy Basic Flight Training, Ottumwa, Iowa.

University of Wisconsin before he moved on to Pre-Flight School in Iowa.

After being detained in Wisconsin for nearly a month, Tex joined a new group of cadets for Pre-Flight Training at the University of Iowa. His reputation as an athlete preceded him, and he made the Iowa Pre-Flight Seahawks basketball team. The team played Northwestern University in Chicago Stadium where Tex guarded Otto Graham. Graham is best known as one of the all-time great quarterbacks for the Cleveland Browns in the National Football League, but he was an All-American basketball player, too. "Playing against Otto Graham was a humbling experience," Tex told his Navy colleagues.

Following basketball season, Tex was held over in Iowa City another two weeks. He pole vaulted in the Chicago Relays, placing second to the world record holder Cornelius Warmerdam, who set a world record of 15' 8¼" with a bamboo pole. ▲

From Iowa Pre-Flight School, Tex was assigned to Ottumwa Iowa Naval Air Station for Basic Flight Training in the spring of 1944. "They're really putting us to the test," Tex told friends and family. "We're flying the Stearman Yellow Peril—what a plane—learning emergency landings (short-field landings), slow flight, and aerobatics. I'm pretty good at aerobatics. I think my pole

Operational Training in Sanford, Florida, 1945, Experimental Squadron.

Back row: A.L. Engel, M.F. Winter, C.E. Gillette, C.E. Berg.

Kneeling: Instructor Ace Pilot, M.H. Hamilton.

> *There is no easy way to acquire skill. It takes perseverance, determination, willingness to work, and practice. The player who does not have or will not develop these qualities of character will be a liability rather than an asset.*

vaulting experience helps. They've still got me competing. I did the Drake Relays in Des Moines where I won the pole vault and placed second in high jump."

Next was Cabiness Field in Corpus Christi in the fall of 1944. At a field with a carrier shape outlined on it, Tex trained in his first low-wing aircraft, nicknamed the Vultee Vibrator. After much rigorous flight training, he moved up to the famous SNJ Texan Navy trainer plane. He graduated and was commended as an Ensign and received his wings, but he had only begun.

Tex was assigned to Sanford, Florida, for Operational Training. "Today, we'd be called Top Guns," Tex added. "We didn't know it at the time, but we were an experimental group selected to learn combat maneuvers from an 'Ace,' a Navy pilot who had returned from World War II combat in the Pacific."

The Ace pilot taught special dog fight tactics and gunnery runs as Tex and his group learned to fly F4Fs, the Navy's top small carrier-based fighter plane. Practicing overhead gunnery runs, Tex would gain altitude high above the target sleeve pulled by a low-flying aircraft, roll the plane over on its back, drop the plane's nose, and pick up the target in his sights. He would blast away, shooting at the target as long as possible. He would dive down beyond the target to begin another "run."

On one such run, Tex descended as planned, with his machine gun blasting away. But he gained too much speed in the

F4F fighter aircraft, called Wildcats, flying
in formation.

"Tex was a Navy fighter pilot during World War II. I only learned that years later. Although he knew I was a fighter pilot in the Air Force for 30 years, he never once mentioned his pilot experience until I asked him about it. He is an authentic, humble human being."

Hog Schuyler
Kansas State University 1954

If you are good— be better.

dive, and, when pulling out of the dive too quickly, blacked out, unconscious in the cockpit. "Pull out of it, Winter. Pull out of it," his instructor yelled into Tex's headphones.

Tex shook his head and blinked hard to read the instrument panel. He was upside down, traveling about three hundred knots at about five hundred feet above the water. In a near-miracle move, he rolled the plane out of upside down attitude, pulled the control stick, and began to climb. Had he pulled back on the stick as his instructor said, he would have flown right into the Atlantic Ocean.

Tex was stunned, as unnerved as he'd ever been. It was a very close call, the worst of several scares he had had during the rigorous training program.

Tex called in. "I'm going back to the base," he said to his instructor.

SS SEEANDBEE

USS WOLVERINE (IX 64)

The *Sable* and the *Wolverine* would be decommissioned when we were finished. It was our last day. I looked around. I was next to last on the downwind leg. *If I take a "wave-off" from a signal officer and circle again,* I thought to myself, *I'll be known as the last guy to land on this carrier.*

On the final approach, I set the Wildcat "in the groove," purposely raised the nose, and added throttle. The signal officer gave me the "too high and too fast" signal. *Good,* I said to myself. *I'll hold this attitude and get a "waveoff."*

But at the very last second, the officer gave me a "cut," which means shut down the throttle. "What is he doing?" I said aloud to an empty cockpit. Since I was trained to follow orders, I cut the throttle. The plane hit the deck and must have bounced ten feet. But somehow, the tail hook caught the arresting cable and the plane jerked to a stop, or I would have ended up in Lake Michigan. Well, my plan didn't work. I had to settle for the next to last landing and the highest bounce. So much for trying to be a hot shot.

SS GREATER BUFFALO

USS SABLE (IX 81)

Side paddlewheel steamers converted into aircraft carriers, the Wolverine (top) and the Sable (bottom).

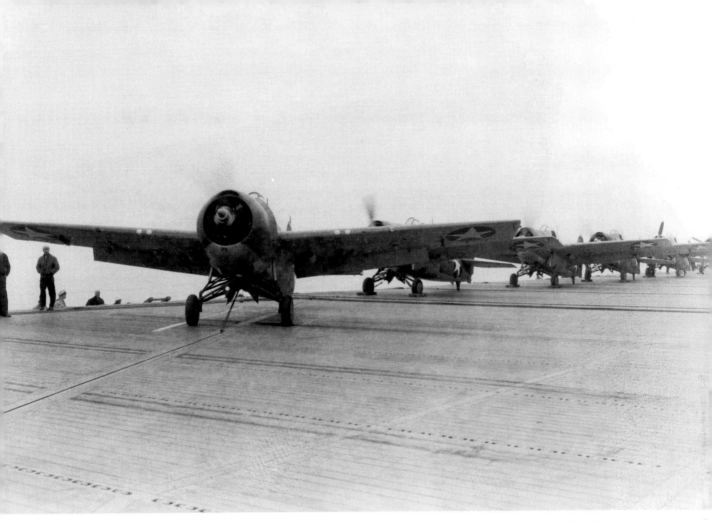

From Operational Training, Tex was sent to Glenwood Illinois Naval Air Station for carrier-landing qualifications in the winter of 1944. Two Great Lakes excursion vessels—flat-bottomed paddle-wheelers—had been converted into carriers with flight decks and operating cables to catch the tail hooks of landing aircraft. Tex practiced landings on carriers called the *Sable* and the *Wolverine* in Lake Michigan. Tex's group was required to make eight "stop and go" landings to qualify as carrier-based fighter pilots.▲

Qualified, experienced, and ready to see action, Tex's group was sent to San Diego in the fall of 1945 as a replacement for a carrier returning from World War II action in the Pacific. While waiting, they continued to practice landings on a training carrier off San Diego. Tex made eighty-two landings, eight of them at night. "Every landing was an incredible high," Tex told Nancy. "They were small carriers. We called them 'Postage Stamps.' You take a deep breath, say a prayer of thanks when you make a landing, and go around again."

Tex completed carrier landings in the F4F aircraft (shown here).

Tex says

As has been said and written: Good, bad, or indifferent, the war's effect upon those who survived naval aviation's greatest challenge marked them for life. I wouldn't take a million dollars for the experience, but you couldn't pay me a million to do it again.

Tex says

I was held over for so many athletic events. When I saw my original group getting their wings and I was still a Cadet, I said no more. Who knows, maybe I would have been sent overseas and seen action in World War II if I'd have said no sooner.

Tex, Cadet (right), and Ernest, Lieutenant Junior Grade, in their Navy uniforms.

Dribble

cut

Pass #2

cut

cut

cut

Pass #1

Begin drill

Next player continues drill

"Ernest was after his little brother all the time. His mother said Fred would have been content to play all day with little cars in his own little dream world. Ernest was always dragging him out, constantly, on his many ventures. Ernest influenced Fred in many good ways."

Nancy Chase Winter
Nancy Winter
Fred "Tex's" wife

Anxious and ready to see action in the Pacific, Tex and his group missed their chances as the war ended before their assigned carrier had returned to San Diego. ▲ Tex felt the letdown as much as anyone. Even though they continued to train, his team was gone.

Tex's brother Ernest, in the same Navy V-5 program two years earlier with six months of training, had flown extraordinary war missions, been shot down over the China Sea, declared missing-in-action, and smuggled to safety by the Chinese. Tex could fly well too, after twenty-four months of training, even if his story lacked the same sizzle. ▲

In December 1945, Tex was sent to Corpus Christi Texas Naval Air Station. He served as a Special Instructor for about two weeks before he was discharged from the Navy and placed on reserve status.

During my last assignment, I took commissioned officers into the air, put the airplanes in unusual attitudes, and evaluated the officers' recovery skills. A Lieutenant Commander and I hiked to a trainer plane on the tarmac of the Corpus Christi Naval Air Station. "Let's get this testing out of the way," the Lieutenant Commander barked. "I want my wings so I can get out of here." He didn't want me to forget that he outranked me several levels.

I started the engine. "Okay," I said. I put the plane on its back into a reverse stall. "Get us out of this."

The Lieutenant Commander messed with knobs, gripped the stick, and fumbled around. First the plane dived, then it stalled again. I waited as long as I could for the Lieutenant Commander to correct course. I put the plane into a stall again, and a third time. I took over just before it was too late each time. I finally said, "You just don't have the orientation for this."

I landed the plane and walked toward the hangar. I approached the chalkboard to record the results. I drew a "down" arrow, the sign which meant the Lieutenant Commander had failed.

The Lieutenant Commander stormed over to the board. "What's this?" he shouted, pointing to the mark that denied him his wings. "You'll live to regret what you just did."

"Well, I don't know about that," I replied, "but I might have saved your life today and in the future."

Tex says I squared up my shoulders, held my head high, and walked toward the airplane to meet another officer. The Navy wasn't that different from a sports team after all, I decided. Every member's best effort was needed, and the Lieutenant Commander hadn't made the cut.

The best talker and the worst flier among the birds is the parrot.

Offensive Build-Up Drills

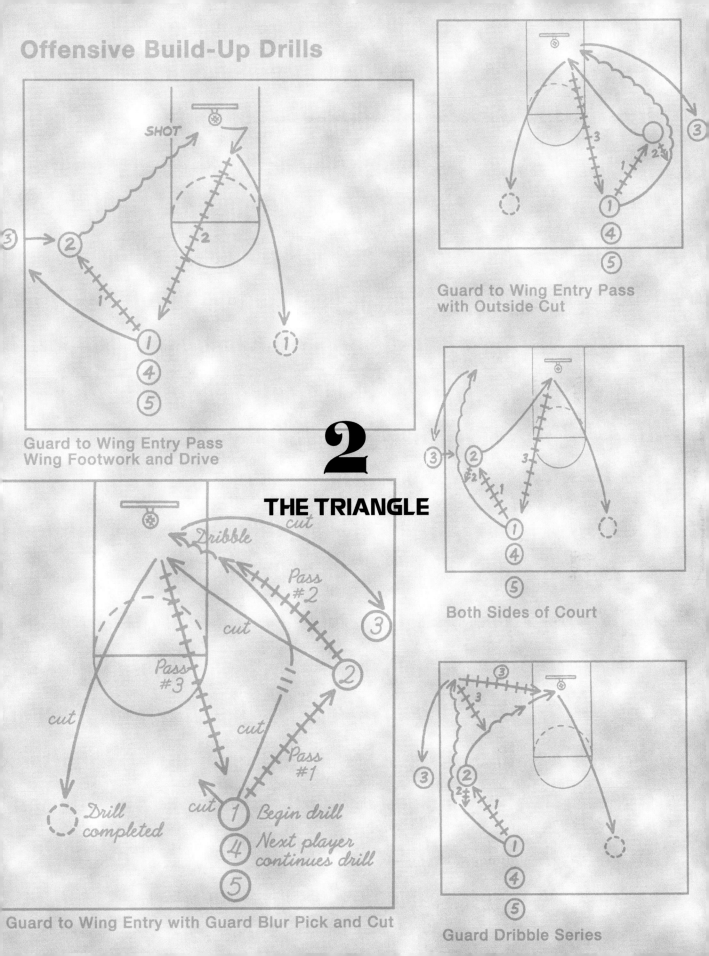

SHOT

Guard to Wing Entry Pass
Wing Footwork and Drive

Guard to Wing Entry Pass
with Outside Cut

Both Sides of Court

2

THE TRIANGLE

cut
Dribble
Pass #2
cut
Pass #3
cut
cut
Pass #1
cut
Drill completed
Begin drill
Next player continues drill

Guard to Wing Entry with Guard Blur Pick and Cut

Guard Dribble Series

State Ka
Sports H o
TEX WIN
Inducte ful

Tex pole vaulting at USC Bovard Field, Los Angeles, California.

Following Tex's discharge from the Navy in December 1945, he went back to Compton Junior College and re-took previously-failed classes, changing those grades from Fs to As. He enrolled at the University of Southern California where he pole-vaulted and played basketball. He became an All-American pole-vaulter with a best collegiate height of 14'4".

Tex's basketball coach, Sam Barry, used a "Center Opposite" offensive pattern reminiscent of what Tex had watched at Huntington Park High School that Coach Jimmy Needles called "Reverse Action." Every day after practice at USC, Tex made more notes on his clipboard, preparing for his own coaching days. Tex finished his Bachelor of Science in physical education degree in the spring of 1947.

Jack Gardner

Tex says

Sam Barry arranged for me to meet Jack Gardner in Lincoln, Nebrasaka where I would be participating in the National AAU Championships for the Los Angeles Athletic Club. I made the trip mainly to meet Gardner, as I had pulled abdominal muscles in an earlier meet and wasn't sure I would be able to vault. I had even borrowed my mother's girdle in hopes it would help, but my dreams of vaulting in the 1948 Olympics evaporated.

Gardner met me in the hotel coffee shop and offered me an opportunity to coach in a Big Six school as my first job. I would be Kansas State's first full-time assistant basketball coach for $3,000 a year.

At Sam Barry's suggestion, Jack Gardner, head basketball coach at Kansas State University, approached Tex. "How about being my assistant?" he asked. Tex was glad to consider this rare opportunity to have his own freshman team as his first coaching job out of college.

Gardner too had played for Sam Barry at USC in the early 1930s. Tex recognized a chance to learn more triangle alignment ideas. He said yes to the offer.▲

Tex married Nancy July 11, 1946. They packed everything they owned into the new Studebaker Nancy's parents had given them as a wedding gift. They moved to Kansas during a scorching hot August in 1947, leaving cool California behind. They arrived in Manhattan at night. Deafening Kansas cicada sounds greeted them. "What have we gotten ourselves into?" Tex asked Nancy.

Tex and Nancy Bohnenkamp were married in LeGrande, Oregon, at the First Presbyterian Church.

Recruit Ernie Barrett
with Coach Gardner.

Tex says

My first day on the job, Gardner says, "I want to see what kind of recruiter you are. The best high school player in Kansas lives in Wellington. See if you can get him." Ernie Barrett was headed for Oklahoma State where his coach had played for Coach Hank Iba. I worked hard on Ernie and his parents. Whatever it took.

Ernie, my first recruit, one of our best players, became an All-American, my assistant coach, Kansas State's Athletic Director, and lifetime advocate for the school, known as Mr. K-State.

Then we signed Jack Stone that I knew from AAU connections in California. Stone knew Eddie Head and told me, "Tex, this guy can really play."

I had played against Eddie too. I could not get a shot off him. He was amazing. I'd beat him on a dribble. I'd get in for a lay-up, and there he was, blocking my shot. I'd say he was the most underrated player we ever had.

My second year, Lew Hitch transferred in. We got Dick Knostman, another top Kansas high school player, and South Dakota's best player, Jim Iverson. And to me, that was the start of one of the best basketball programs in the country.

Tex with Coach Gardner.

As Gardner's assistant, Tex recruited players. He looked for students with first, good positive character traits; and second, the ability to learn motor skills. He wanted players who would work hard on the basketball court. ▲

Gardner and Winter's team won the 1948 Big Six championship, the first conference title for Kansas State since 1919. They finished the season with 22 wins and 6 losses, took fourth in the NCAA Tournament, and earned the school's first national ranking. Gardner told Tex, "You're finding players with 'heart'."

The Wildcats finished the 1949-50 season with 17 wins and 7 losses and tied for the Big Six Conference title. They won the conference title the next year as well as the Western NCAA Regionals. With leading-scorer Barrett injured, they lost to the University of Kentucky in the National Championship game.

Kansas State Freshmen Team, 1947 with Coach Winter as their first full-time assistant coach.

Back row: Coach Winter, Don Rogers, Henry Specht, Ed Head, Bernard William, Bob Blabau, Coach Gardner.

Middle row: Dick Johnson, Bill Dresser, Walter Way, Glen Channell, Jack Stone, Ernie Barrett, Milt Boznic.

Front row: Dan Upson, Bill Boner, Bill Boldenow, Norm Mortimer, Buddy Tomlins, Don Button.

1951-52.
Marquette University Basketball

Tex says I was eager to get started on my own. First, I drilled in the skills I had learned at Kansas State and then recruited a fine team.

Our first game was with Ripon, a small school nearby. We played at our old Claybourne Street Gymnasium. I had my team in the locker room, getting them ready to play. In fact, I was overly eager, wanting to be sure they were prepared. Consequently, I didn't get the team out onto the floor in time. I started my career as head coach with a technical foul because we were late. *Great beginning*, I told myself.

Marquette University Varsity Team 1952.

Back Row: Don Marek, Pete Basarich, Russ Wittberger, Rube Schulz, Grant Wittberger, Dale Sevcik, John Puk, Jerry O'Brien.

Middle Row: Coach Winter, Syl Bado, Charles Dunn, Dick Schwab, John Jansky, Ray Kotz, John Powers, Gene Schramka, Assistant Coach Jack Nagle.

Front row: Manager George Erwin, Cliff DeCeault, Ralph Wilson, Bob VanVooren, Erich Siverling, Doug Gill, Glenn Sievers, Bob Walczak.

Tex Winter, youngest head coach
of an NCAA Division I team, 1951.

Coach Bill Chandler and Tex, when they were coach
and player during Navy War Training School at
Marquette University.

While at the NCAA Tournament, Tex visited with
Bill Chandler, a coach for whom he had played in the Navy.
Chandler was retiring from Marquette University in Milwaukee,
Wisconsin the next season and recommended Tex for the
Marquette job. After four years as Gardner's assistant at Kansas
State, at age 28, Tex had a chance to become the youngest head
coach of a Division I NCAA school.

Tex remembered how Chandler and his commander, Chuck
Taylor, had talked to him about his basketball playing ability,
encouraging him with praise. He was flattered that Chandler
and Taylor had followed his career so closely. Tex took the position. ▲

"Tex took underclassmen to the National Catholic Invitational Tournament in 1952. This was not a popular move to leave upper-classmen behind. However, Tex was right, because with those players, he won the tournament. Then he made a special trip to Milwaukee in 2002 to attend our fiftieth anniversary celebration of winning that 1952 tournament. He was still the same old good guy, saying nice things about Marquette."

Gene Schramka

Gene Schramka
Marquette 1952

Tex says

One of our Marquette guys went in for a game-winning layup. A University of Wisconsin player punched the ball out of the basket from underneath the goal. Neither of the officials saw it. But their coach, Bud Foster, saw it. I went down to the scorer's bench, complaining. Foster said, "I can't comment." I didn't blame him, but that probably cost us the game. When we played them again in Milwaukee, we won, 51-47 on December 22, 1951. It was a big, big win for us and for me as a very young coach.

Marquette University, 50th Reunion of team that won Catholic Invitational Tournament.

Back row: Syl Bado, Erich Siverling, Jerry O'Brien, John Powers, John Puk, Gene Schramka, Glenn Sievers, Pete Basarich, Dick Schwab, John Jansky, Rube Schulz, Grant Wittberger, Dale Sevcik, Charles Dunn, Russ Wittberger.

Front row: Manager Bill Isaacson, Coach Tex Winter, Bob Walczak, Bob VanVooren.

The Winter Family in 1956.
Nancy holding Brian; Russ, Tex, and Chris.

Two years later, Jack Gardner left Kansas State. Tex was asked to replace him. "I'll have to think about it," Tex told the Athletic Director, Moon Mullins. "I have recruited some very good players at Marquette. We're doing well, and I'm building for the future."▲

As Tex weighed his choices, he thought he would like the challenge of returning to build a program that he had helped start, although he expected the transition to be rocky. He hated to leave a program with such good prospects, but he also would be leaving a good team for his successor, Jack Nagle, his able assistant at Marquette. He took the Kansas State job.

Tex and Nancy moved back to Manhattan, Kansas, and settled in. Tex and Nancy's first son, Russell, was born in 1950 when Tex was assistant to Gardner. Their second son, Christopher, was born in 1953 in Milwaukee, Wisconsin, the year Tex returned to Kansas State as head coach; and their third son, Brian, in 1955, in Manhattan, which became home to the Winter family.

Tex made a plan for Kansas State's future, as he had done at Marquette. Expectations were high, given the records Gardner had built. Fans believed Tex would continue the tradition, even

Kansas State was spoiled with Gardner's great teams. Fans' expectations ruled the day, and they were really high. When they brought me back, they thought things would just continue, but Gardner took players with him. It was a painful time for me. I could go way back and say my mother didn't even want me at first, because she didn't know how she was going to take care of twins. That changed and I became very close to my mother, but my story was still there. Now, signs in Manhattan told me to go away. I had to make a decision about whether to stay in coaching and at Kansas State. But the biggest decision was whether I would become a quitter. Obviously, I decided not to quit, and that decision to stick things out stayed with me the rest of my life. I'm glad it worked out the way it did, because by the time we took the league title in 1956 and earned our first national ranking, I had built up confidence in my coaching ability.

Tex says

"His passion for the game along with his resilience and strength of character has enabled him to continue the road trips, recruiting, separation from family, and pressures of all kinds, which coaches experience."

Charlie Dunn
Charlie Dunn
Marquette University

Tex says

A challenge awaiting me at Kansas State was the long-standing rivalry with Kansas University. I admired the team and especially the coach, Dr. Phog Allen (a licensed chiropractor). He had built an outstanding program at Kansas University. Phog had played under Dr. James Naismith, inventor of the game of basketball. But I dared to disagree with Phog about a burning issue of the day—the height of the basketball goal. "Twelve-foot baskets give the big man an advantage at the game," I told him. Allen favored twelve-foot baskets. I did not. Ten-foot baskets remained.

In my mind, I again question the height of the basket for today's players. The average height of a basketball player in the 1940s and 1950s was about 6'2". Today's average basketball player is 6'6". To maintain the same ratio of basket to player, today's goals should be about 10'6" tall.

> *There are two sides to everything—including a sheet of flypaper. But it makes a lot of difference to the fly which side he is on.*

though Gardner took players, including a sophomore ranked as the best in the Big Seven Conference, with him to the University of Utah. He almost persuaded two leading tall players to go with him too. "I didn't realize how bare he had left the cupboard until I got here," Tex told his assistants. "I left far better personnel behind at Marquette."

Fortunately, two of his freshman Marquette recruits—Pachin Vincens and Fritz Schneider—decided to transfer with him.

Tex's first two seasons as head coach at Kansas State ended in twin records—11 wins and 10 losses. Expectations were unrealistic, and fans became dissatisfied. They wanted more victories, especially against Kansas University, their biggest rival. ▲ Tex tried to explain his vision. But by the end of the 1955 season, fans ran out of patience. Someone put up banners on campus that read, "Spring is here—Winter must go." ▲

Tex faced a crossroads in his career. Should he quit or stick it out? He promised himself he would think long and hard about this important decision. He had faced difficulties before—his dad's death, moving to California, losing out on World War II action in the Navy. He remembered his strong desire to teach and coach, gathered up his skills to recognize basketball savvy, and did what he knew best. He made a plan and went looking for more talented players, with character, to develop.

> "Tex's first order of business at Marquette was to improve the recruiting and bring in a different level of talent. This he did so effectively that by the time his first recruits were seniors, Marquette went 24 and 3 and earned their way to the NCAA Tournament and defeated Kentucky. All of this was undreamed of before Tex."
>
> *C. William Isaacson*
> Bill Isaacson
> Marquette University

Kansas State Varsity Team, 1955–56.

Back Row: Larry Fischer, Bob Jedwabny, Joe Powell, Jack Parr, Wayne Hutchins, Charles Hollinger, Henry Pierce.

Middle Row: Coach Winter, Fritz Schneider, Hayden Abbott, Bill Laude, Dick Stone, Dean Plagge, Roy DeWitz, Assistant Coach Howie Shannon.

Front row: Warren Bullock, Pachin Vicens, Don Matuszak, Don Richards, Jack Kiddoo, Eddie Wallace, Gene Wilson, Manager Bob Boyd.

Tex says

At the end of the 1955–56 season, we had a one-game conference lead over Kansas University, one that would disappear if we lost to them. Furthermore, Coach Allen was being forced into retirement at age seventy by an obscure tenure rule. Kansas University looked forward to winning over us one more time to salute their coach at his last game.

We trailed by only eight points at half-time. "You're fired up," I told my team. "You can do it. Play as a team. Keep the floor spaced and move the ball."

My Wildcats came storming back and sealed the Big Seven Championship over Kansas University. This was a highlight of my coaching career. Allen was gracious in our defeat of his team. But he had always been gracious to me. He sent me letters congratulating me on the fine job of coaching he thought I was doing. He was truly a gentleman.

Tex's Triangle

By Frederick C. Klein

The Triangle's basic setup—the one that gives it its name—involves putting three players on the same side of the lane—one near the sideline, one near the free-throw circle and one down low, near the basket. The player with the ball can drive to the hoop or shoot if those opportunities present themselves, or pass, usually to one of his triangle mates. Once he passes, he can move to the hoop for a return pass, or to an unoccupied part of the court. In the latter case, the triangle re-forms around the new ball handler, who repeats the same options.

The overloading of one side of the floor is a key to the system's effectiveness. "It's a basic way to attack a zone defense," Mr. Winter says. Reminded that NBA rules prohibit zones, he merely shrugs.

But that's not all there is to it. The proper spacing of offensive players—15 to 18 feet apart—is vital. So is the interchangeability of positions, with centers, say operating from the outside or the corners as often as from around the basket. So, too, according to the coach, is the players' ability to think on their feet.

"The defense doesn't just stand there while we do our things, so we have to be able to read it and react," he said. "It's a constant process of adjustment that, when it works, leads to the small advantages that can lead to baskets."

In the lingo of the times, Mr. Winter calls the triangle an "equal opportunity" system that's supposed to produce scoring chances for every player. It's that part about it that raises the most eyebrows. It that's true, people ask, why do most of the opportunities—and points—fall to [one or two players]?

Knowing that in basketball, as in other endeavors, opportunities may be equal but ability isn't, Mr. Winter smiles at this query. "The triangle can produce the shots, but it can't make them go in," he says.

The Wall Street Journal Friday, February 14, 1997.

Tex's addition of new players—Hayden Abbott, Roy DeWitz, Larry Fischer, Don Matuzak, Jack Parr, Dean Plagge, and Don Richards—made fans happier. But the Wildcats still were losing to Kansas University—five times in a row, in fact.

Tex worked his Wildcats hard. Using his offensive plan, he focused on fundamentals—passing, shooting, and dribbling the ball. "You can do it," Tex told his Wildcats during half time against Kansas University. "Remember, it's a team game. Keep yourselves spaced about fifteen feet apart and move the ball." ▲

It was Coach Allen's last game of his long Kansas University career and the last regular season game, one that decided the Big Seven title. Schneider, Tex's transfer from Marquette, scored thirty-six points and Parr pulled down sixteen rebounds for a win of 79-68. It was the turning point in Tex's coaching career.

The Wildcats took the 1956 league title and were ranked #1 in the nation several times during the next season, their first national ranking with Tex as head coach. Kansas State had regained its once proud tradition as a national power.

Dr. Phog Allen lettered in basketball under Dr. James Naismith. Allen coached at Kansas University 1908–1909, and 1920–1956.

"I came from a low income background. My folks sat me down and said, 'There's this much for college. It goes to your sister. You're on your own.' I wouldn't have seen a college door except for Tex Winter and the athletic scholarship he made possible for me."

Robert L. Boozer

Bob Boozer
Kansas State University 1959

Dr. James Naismith developed a new game in 1891 for Springfield, Massachusetts YMCA Training School students between football and baseball seasons using peach baskets and a soccer ball.

The first basketball, a rubber bladder covered with leather and laced with a shoestring.

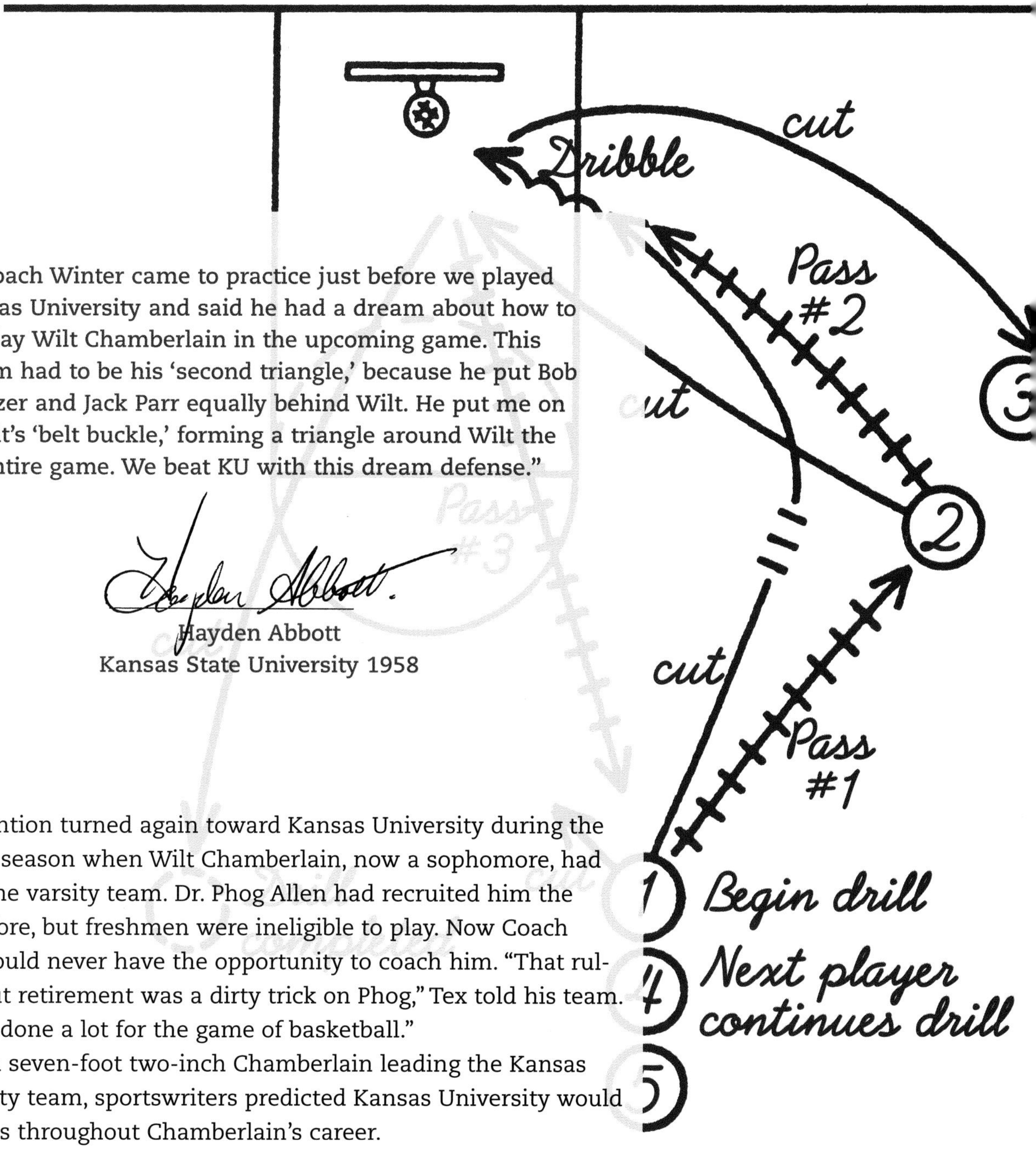

The diagram labels: cut, Dribble, Pass #2, cut, cut, Pass #1, 2, 3

> "Coach Winter came to practice just before we played Kansas University and said he had a dream about how to play Wilt Chamberlain in the upcoming game. This dream had to be his 'second triangle,' because he put Bob Boozer and Jack Parr equally behind Wilt. He put me on Wilt's 'belt buckle,' forming a triangle around Wilt the entire game. We beat KU with this dream defense."

Hayden Abbott
Hayden Abbott
Kansas State University 1958

1 Begin drill
4 Next player continues drill
5

Attention turned again toward Kansas University during the 1956–57 season when Wilt Chamberlain, now a sophomore, had joined the varsity team. Dr. Phog Allen had recruited him the year before, but freshmen were ineligible to play. Now Coach Allen would never have the opportunity to coach him. "That ruling about retirement was a dirty trick on Phog," Tex told his team. "He has done a lot for the game of basketball."

With seven-foot two-inch Chamberlain leading the Kansas University team, sportswriters predicted Kansas University would win titles throughout Chamberlain's career.

Tex had recruited another big man, Bob Boozer at six-foot eight-inches, the year before. Boozer, along with Jack Parr at six-foot nine-inches, was now eligible to help beat Kansas University.

After losing to Kansas University early in the 1957–58 season, the Wildcats again met Kansas University for a game that changed the momentum of the season. The Wildcats double-teamed Chamberlain and led by thirteen points at the half. Chamberlain's easy lay-in for a win at the end of the first

"My parents attended only one game during my college career. I got off the bench only during warm-ups and time-outs. In the 1958 regionals, I played the entire second half and all the overtime in the championship game against Cincinnati. Nobody said life was fair, and we must adjust to circumstances. Tex helped me learn that."

Larry Fischer
Kansas State University 1958

Tex says

This being the era before the shot clock, many coped with Chamberlain and the Kansas University team by stalling their way through games.

I disagreed. I believed that holding the ball was against the integrity of the game. But I did agree with other rule changes, largely aimed at players as tall as Chamberlain. I was chairman of the National Association of Basketball Coaches Rules Recommendations Committee at the time.

Chamberlain called me "the little guy from Kansas State who tried to get rid of me." I don't think he even knew my name. I said you had to live the Wilt Chamberlain experience to fully realize his impact. He changed the game—and the rules.

Kansas State Edges Cincinnati, 83 to 80

Third-ranked Kansas State Wildcats and the second-rated Bearcats of Cincinnati treated the crowd of 17,000 to as thrilling a basketball game as has ever been played in this area.

The score was tied 12 times and the biggest lead enjoyed by either team was a eight-point margin by the Big Eight champions shortly after the midway point of the second half.

Oscar Robertson, who made eight of 12 field goal attempts and 18 points in the first half, took charge and personally drove Cincinnati into a 40-39 lead at half time.

The second half was a nip and tuck affair with the score tied six times before K-State took the lead with eight minutes to play.

Robertson, held in check in the early part of the second period, finally found the range again and joined with teammate Connie Dierking to tie the score at 69-all.

Dierking committed his fifth personal a second later and the Wildcats proceeded to cash in consistently from the foul line.

Trailing by one point at 74-73 after Roberston connected on a field goal and two free throws with one second

to go, Oscar drove for the basket and was fouled.

The Cinncinati ace tied the score at 74-all with his first free throw but missed the one which would have sent them off the court as victors in regulation.

Robertson fouled out with one minute gone in the overtime session, and with teammate Dierking also on the sidelines, the Missouri Valley champions had no answer for the well-balanced attack of the Big Eight champions.

Salina Journal March 16, 1958

Kansas State Varsity Team 1957–58.

Back Row: Freshman Coach Howie Shannon, Steve Douglas, Bob Boozer, Jack Parr, Wally Frank, Howard Rice, Larry Fischer, Bill Laude.

Middle Row: Glen Long, Dean Plagge, Bob Graham, Hayden Abbott, Bob Merten, Roy DeWitz, Coach Winter.

Front Row: Manager John Stone, Don Matuszak, Don Richards, Sonny Ballard, Jim Holwerda, Bill Guthridge.

overtime was blocked by Jack Parr. Even though he and Boozer fouled out during the second overtime, the Wildcat team maintained the momentum to win 79–75. Fans went crazy. So did Tex. Chamberlain left Kansas University to join the Globetrotters. ▲

Tex's Wildcats traveled to the NCAA tournament after overcoming Cincinnati and beating Oklahoma State University to win the Midwest Regionals before losing to Seattle. "We finished 22–5 and were ranked #1 in the nation several times during the season," Tex said. "That gave us the impetus to work hard. We played against Oscar Robertson with the University of Cincinnati, Wilt Chamberlain at Kansas University, and Elgin Baylor at Seattle, three first-team All-Americans, along with Bob Boozer and Jerry West. One of the highlights of my career and Kansas State's tradition of basketball was our 1958 win over Cincinnati and Oscar Robertson in the NCAA Midwest Regionals. *Sports Illustrated* called it the College Game of the Year."

cut

Pass #1

1 Begin drill

4 Next player continues drill

5

United Press Tabs Tex As Top Coach

Coach Tex Winter, of the Kansas State Wildcats, today was named Basketball Coach of the Year by the United Press wire service, in a poll of 236 UP sports writers and sports casters.

Winter, who will send his team against Cincinnati tonight in the NCAA Regionals at Lawrence, received 74 votes to 42 by runner-up, Fred Schaus, of West Virginia. Phil Woolpert, of San Francisco, a two-time recipient of the award, was third with 19.

Tex says

The Triangle is about player and ball movement based on spacing on the floor with a purpose. It replaces the idea of head-to-head defense by finding and taking advantage of the defense's weaknesses. When the defense spreads out to prevent some offensive move, Triangle players instinctively adjust with cuts and passes to find a better shot.

Kansas State Varsity 1958–59

Back Row: Assistant Coach Howie Shannon, Glen Long, Wally Frank, Bob Boozer, Steve Douglas, Coach Winter.

Middle Row: Gary Balding, Bob Graham, Jerry Johnson, Sonny Ballard.

Front Row: Bill Guthridge, Jack Whittier, Don Matuszak, Jim Holwerda, Manager Don Ungerer.

Not shown: Glenn Hamilton, Mickey Heinz, Ced Price, Howard Rice, Assistant Coach Ernie Barrett.

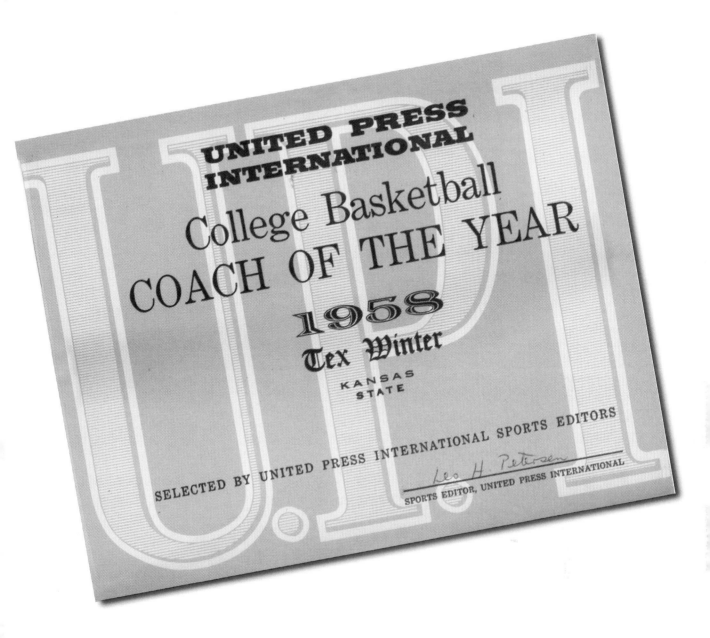

UNITED PRESS INTERNATIONAL

College Basketball
COACH OF THE YEAR

1958
Tex Winter
KANSAS STATE

SELECTED BY UNITED PRESS INTERNATIONAL SPORTS EDITORS

Leo H. Petersen

SPORTS EDITOR, UNITED PRESS INTERNATIONAL

United Press International honored Tex with the Coach of the Year award. He was also named NCAA Coach of the Year, the youngest Division I coach to receive that honor. He gave his players the credit. "It is a team game, you know."

The next year Tex's team held onto a #1 national ranking throughout the season, winning twenty-one games straight after losing an early game to Brigham Young University. "We won over Kansas University twice—once on our home court for the first time in my career—swept the Big Eight title with 14 wins and no losses, lost to Cincinnati in the Midwest Regionals, and finished the season 25–2," Tex said. "Those were exciting times, another year when I said that this was my best team yet."

Tex, right, and older brother Ernest, play cards in 1963.

My brother Ernest, a dentist in Lawton, Oklahoma, was totally wrapped up in my career. He pushed me from the time our dad died. He set me on the straight and narrow. That was a good thing, because in Southern California, I had many temptations.

During ball games, Ernest would sit right behind me and say, "Freck, do this. Freck, do that."

During a game between Kansas State and Oklahoma, Ernest followed me and the team to the locker room during half time. Usually, I would have asked him to leave, but I didn't this time. I went to the board to draw up plans for second half. He started talking to the players and left the locker room with them, closing the door. I got to the door, and it was locked. By the time I pounded on the door loud enough to get someone to open it, Ernest was in the huddle with the players, ready to send them out for the tip-off. Nobody realized I wasn't there until I showed up. We did win the game.

In 1964, when Ernest failed to hear a fire truck's siren, his car was hit broadside, and he was killed. It was almost like losing my father all over again. He was always full of advice and my biggest critic, but he was also my **Tex says** best supporter. I always tried to please him, and it wasn't easy.

68

Tex and Nancy with their three
sons: Russ, Brian, and Chris.

By 1968, Tex had coached at
Kansas State for nineteen years,
four as assistant coach and fifteen as head coach. ▲ The
Winter sons attended Manhattan, Kansas schools and helped
their dad build a cozy home. Nancy built life-long friendships.

Tex builds a new
home for his family
in Manhattan,
Kansas.

Tex organized his ideas and wrote a book about the Triangle,
entitled *Triple-Post Offense*, published by Prentice-Hall, Inc. in
1963. Along with clear-cut techniques and specific plans for practices, the book had sections about relaxation, concentration,
temperament, and discipline.

"I'm thinking about a change," Tex told Cotton Fitzsimmons,
his assistant coach at the end of the 1967–68 season. "I'm going
to recommend you for my job. You're a head coach by nature.
You're ready for this team."

"Don't go yet," Fitzsimmons answered. "Stay one more year, at
least."

Big 8 Champs — Midwest NCAA Champs Fourth NCAA Finals

1963-64

Kansas State Varsity 1963–64

Back Row: Lou Poma, Dave Nelson, Joe Gottfrid, Roger Suttner, Gary Williams, Jim Hoffman, Willie Murrell.

Middle Row: Assistant Coach Howie Shannon, Dick Barnard, Larry Berger, Jeff Simons, Ron Paradis, Assistant Coach Bill Guthridge, Coach Winter.

Front Row: Manager Jerry Simpson, Bill Gettler, Max Moss, Sammy Robinson, Bob McConnell, Trainer Porky Morgan.

Tex says

Many of my players and fellow coaches have asked why I didn't stay at Kansas State for the rest of my coaching career. There are many reasons. I had an able assistant coach, Cotton Fitzsimmons, who was ready for the spotlight. I like change—always have—and recruiting in the Midwest had become really tough. So now, this far down the road, I sometimes wonder what my career record might have been if I had stayed. Even if I took the number of wins of my successors through the years, I would have had an impressive number of wins, like hardly any other college coach. But also I would have been forced into retirement at age seventy, and I've coached fourteen years longer than that already. I would have missed out on many good years with exceptional players in other colleges and in the pros. I feel I have been so blessed. No regrets.

Tex Winter at K-State (1954–68)

Year	Overall	Big 7/8 (finish)
1954	11–10	5–7 (4th-t)
1955	11–10	6–6 (3rd-t)
1956	17–8	9–3 (1st), NCAA Tournament
1957	15–8	8–4 (2nd)
1958	22–5	10–2 (1st), NCAA Final Four
1959	25–2	14–0 (1st), Ranked 1st AP & UPI
1960	16–10	10–4 (1st-t)
1961	23–4	13–1 (1st), NCAA Tournament
1962	22–3	12–2 (2nd), Ranked 5th UPI, 6th AP
1963	16–9	11–3 (1st-t)
1964	22–7	12–2 (1st), NCAA Final Four
1965	12–13	5–9 (6th-t)
1966	14–11	9–5 (3rd)
1967	17–8	9–5 (4th)
1968	19–9	11–3 (1st), NCAA Tournament
Totals	262–117	144–55

Kansas State University Sports Information

Coach Cotton Fitzsimmons learning from Coach Tex.

Tex heard his plea, but needed to pay attention to his own instincts. He believed Fitzsimmons would be a good replacement. Tex felt he was getting a little stale, saying the same things over and over at end-of-season banquets and during fan club presentations. He also faced the fact that recruiting had become very difficult.

"I've worked hard at this Kansas State program," Tex told friends. "We have just won the eighth conference championship in my fifteen years as head coach. I feel that it will be very tough to repeat what we have just done. I hope someone else can."

Tex considered another factor. The football program was gearing up, using all the resources possible, and Tex felt the timing for a change was right for both programs.

Tex departed Kansas State with one of the best records in college basketball (both wins and losses and the highest winning percentage—69.1%—at Kansas State). He left an opportunity to build an astounding college coaching career record. "That potential was not important to me at the time," Tex reflected later. "Look at what has happened in the meantime. Things turned out fine. I haven't looked back, but I have wondered." ▲

At Kansas State, my Wildcats had met Wooden's Bruins in a 1964 NCAA Final Four game. I remember how the score see-sawed back and forth. When we led by five points with five minutes left in the game, the Bruins cheerleaders arrived after being delayed by travel problems. I watched as they jumped into the excitement and fired up the crowd. In the meantime, two of our shots went into the basket only to spin back out. The Bruins grabbed the opportunity and pulled away to win 90–84. It was a heart-breaking loss. "We won it on the floor," our fans said as they tried to make sense of the score, "but we lost it at the free-throw line—scoring ten of twenty-one."

I thought we should have won the game. I was disappointed that we lost, but I was very proud of the way we played. I really wanted to beat Wooden's team, which I never did. But he definitely practiced team concepts. Our teaching methods were a lot alike too. I had my Triangle ideas in place, even written in my book, before he won any of his championships. Maybe he learned something from me.

Tex says

Wooden's UCLA Bruins went on to win their first national championship in 1964 and nine more national championships in the next eleven seasons. I often wondered how different things might have been for both programs if we had won that game. I'll never know, but the setback did change things. My Wildcats did not do well the next year.

"Dad had a real sense of responsibility and dedication to his family. He would schedule time with each of us sons. He did a weekly coach's broadcast about an hour's trip away from home. He would take one of us. He'd engage us, talk with us, driving in the dark. He's a remarkable man, unpretentious. I think he allows himself to be taken advantage of because he believes in people's goodness so much."

Russ Winter

Russ Winter
Fred "Tex's" oldest son

In the fall of 1968, Tex moved to Seattle to lead the University of Washington's basketball program. "Let's go back to the west coast, near your parents in LaGrande, Oregon. They're getting older and could use our help," Tex told Nancy.

The family bought a home on Mercer Island, a ferry ride from Seattle, Washington. Russ, Chris, and Brian, now teenagers, enjoyed the *Jolly Roger* motor boat Tex bought for the family. Tex often boated to the university, ten miles across Lake Washington, at fifty miles an hour with no windshield.

At the University of Washington, Tex went head-to-head with John Wooden's UCLA championship Bruins team. Wooden had built a national winning reputation with his aggressive methods of recruiting and coaching. He drove his players, including the team's leader, Lew Alcindor, who adopted his new Muslim name, Kareem Abdul-Jabbar, after the 1967-68 season. Tex wanted to win too, but his approaches were different from Wooden's. "However, our overall philosophies about team play are more alike than different," Tex told colleagues. ▲

31 Jay Bond C

George "Whistle" Davidson

Tex Winter

Lynn Nance

45 Marc Wallace F

HUSKIES

34 Van Bye F

14 Bruce Case G

33 Steve Hawes F-C

23 George Irvine F

22 Rafael Stone G

30 Dave West G

11 Dave Willenborg G

40 Ken Krell F

20 Chris Smith G

10 Paul Tillman F

12 Mike Tryoer G

32 Pat Woolcock G-F

Tex's team at the University of Washington, 1970–71.

Jimmy Needles, back center, with his Loyola University players Phil Woolpert, left; and Pete Newell, right.

Tex says

I first met Pete Newell when he and his Loyola of Los Angeles team practiced evenings in my high school gymnasium. It was Loyola's coach, Jimmy Needles, who ran the "reverse action" offense, giving me my first ideas about the Triangle Offense.

Pete and I stayed in touch through the years. As general manager for the San Diego Rockets NBA team, Newell asked me to become the Rockets head coach for the 1971–72 season. I took the job. Newell and I made a five-year plan. I deeply respected him and expected that together we would be successful. The family welcomed a return to the west coast, and I looked forward to a great challenge.

"Tex worked with the first structured offense in the history of basketball. The Triple Post Offense is his claim to fame. He refined it, as we all have. His offense has a name that has gained well-deserved recognition. The endurance shows after all these years."

Pete Newell

Pete Newell
Big Man Camps, Las Vegas

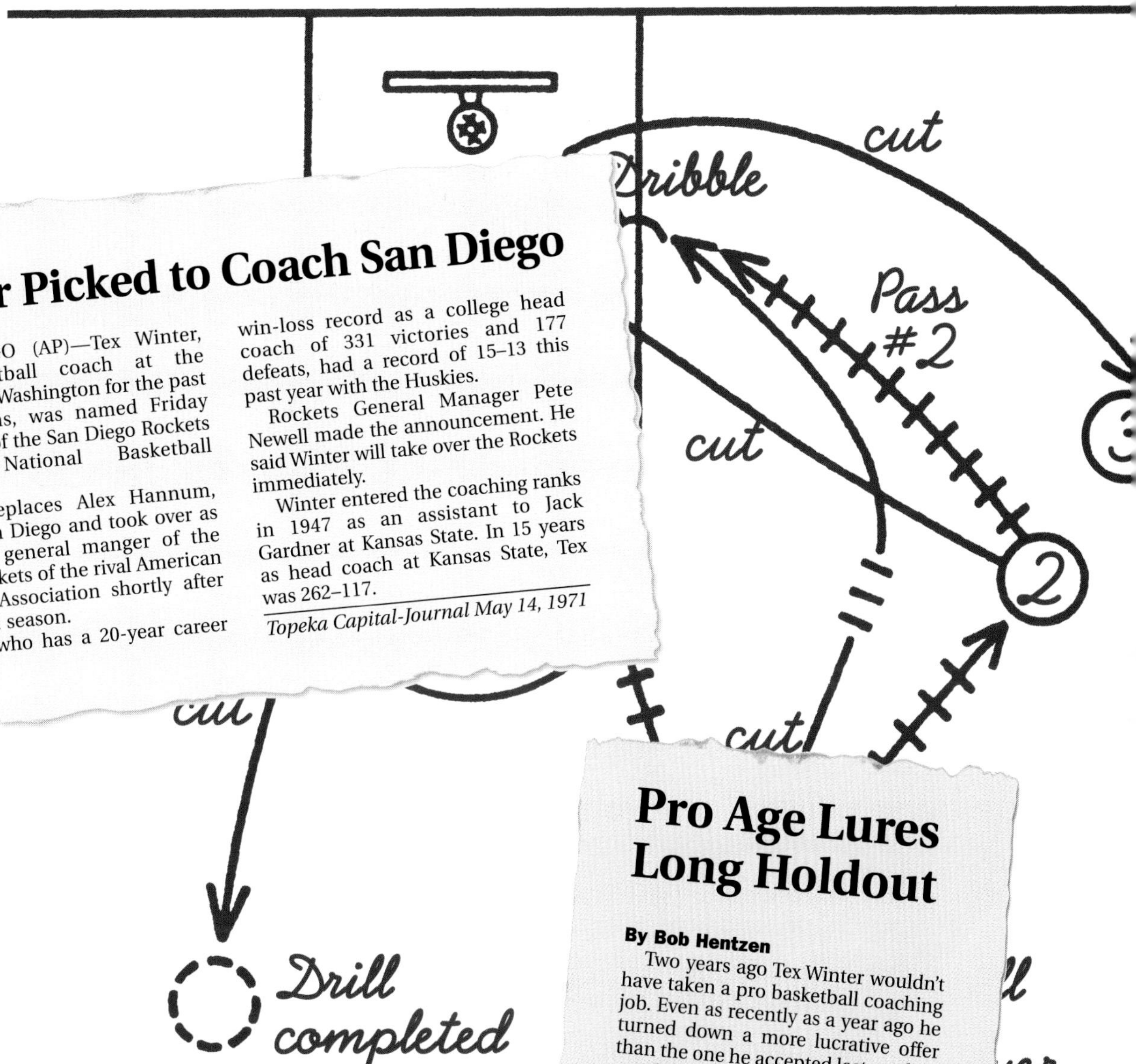

Dribble

cut

Pass #2

cut

cut

cut

cut

○ Drill
completed

Tex visited with his successor at Kansas State, Cotton Fitzsimmons, who had moved to the National Basketball Association (NBA) as coach of the Phoenix Suns after two years as Kansas State's head coach. Fitzsimmons told Tex the Triangle would work in the pros, and that Tex might enjoy working with larger, more experienced players. Tex had had pro coaching offers before, but now he was tempted. Tex signed on with the San Diego Rockets. ▲

Within a month, the Rockets changed owner-ship and were moved to Houston, becoming the Houston Rockets. They had no home arena, and

> *To lose your temper because of somebody else is to punish yourself for another's shortcomings.*

After losing the first six games of the season, I realized that I had inherited a more difficult situation than I could have imagined.

After a pitiful 2–16 season start, the Rockets played the last part of the season 28–26. This included beating the Los Angeles Lakers with Jerry West, Wilt Chamberlain, and Elgin Baylor. The Rockets's performance proved to me that the Rockets could compete with any team. Once the players matured a bit and learned to play together, it made quite a difference. I wished I could wipe out the first two months.

Since Pete Newell did not move to Houston as general manager, the Rockets hired Ray Patterson, former general manager with the Milwaukee Bucks. "We've had a very good first year under the circumstances," he told me. He also let me know that Tom Nissalke, an assistant coach with his former team, would be his choice as the next Rockets coach.

Tex says I wasn't bitter about leaving pro ball. I thought of myself as an educator and there's just not that much opportunity to have influence on young men in pro ball. It was a good experience, and I believe it made me a better coach.

Houston Rockets 1971–72

Standing: Trainer Dick Vandervoort, Radio Broadcaster Art Eckman, Dick Gibbs, Rudy Tomjanovich, Elvin Hayes, Dick Cunningham, Cliff Meely, Greg Smith, Coach Winter.

Kneeling: Calvin Murphy, John Vallely, Mike Newlin, Stu Lantz, John Egan.

1) Begin drill

4) Next player continues drill

5)

instead, played in seven different locations around Texas. The general manager did not make the move with the Rockets. This was not the arrangement Tex had bargained for. Management made decisions without informing Tex. Some players opposed Tex's ideas about the Triangle, saying that focusing on the fundamentals of the game and team concepts would hurt their individual play and scoring. A new general manager wanted an assistant from the Milwaukee Bucks as his head coach. Tex knew he was on borrowed time. He was ready to return to college ball where he could have more influence over his program. ▲

The Winter era begins today

By David Mark Purdy

Tex Winter, Northwestern's new basketball coach, says that "coaches have a responsibility to the students. It's one of a coach's primary responsibilities to provide a service to students. I plan to do anything I can to do that."

Winter, 51, was officially named head coach Thursday, after a three week search by NU athletic director Tippy Dye. Winter will replace Bard Snyder, who resigned March 12.

In 1968, Winter became head coach at the University of Washington and in 1971 he was hired to coach the San Diego Rockets of the National Basketball Association. The Rockets moved to Houston later that season. Winter coached the Rockets until Jan. 21 of this year, when he was replaced by John Egan, a member of the team.

"I'm looking forward to coming back to college ball," Winter said. "I feel that I'm a teacher type of coach, and you have the opportunity to teach more in college."

Northwestern Daily April 6, 1973

Tex says

My lifetime relationship with Jerry began in the 1950s when he visited me at Kansas State. He loved my Triangle offense ideas. We spent hours watching films while I answered his questions. His goal was to be general manager for an NBA team some day, and he wanted me to mentor young coaches in my Triangle offense with his team.

Jerry Krause

cut

Dribble

cut

Pass #2

cut

③

cut

Pass #3

cut

②

Pass #1

① *Begin drill*

④ *Next player continues drill*

⑤

Tex moved to Northwestern University in Chicago, Illinois, taking with him a ranking of the fourth "winningest" coach in college basketball. He welcomed the chance to work on the college-level again, to teach the basic skills, and to develop players.

Jerry Krause, an acquaintance while Tex was at Kansas State, recruited players for the Chicago Bulls NBA team and lived in the Chicago area. They renewed their friendship over weekly lunches. "You've got the poorest basketball facility in the Big Ten," Krause told Tex.

Krause was talking about McGraw Hall, an arena with old, dirt-packed floors, used for all sports. Folding bleachers made of steel tubing and splintered wood boards sat beneath gray walls and darker gray support beams. The lighting was bad too. Krause was right.

"But I tell my recruits the stands are close to the floor and that makes McGraw attractive for the fans," Tex told Krause. Krause was not convinced. ▲

Winter May Move to Sustain Reputation

By Dan Lauck, Staff Writer

SAN DIEGO—Tex Winter is not a vain man. Never has been. He's gone two months with adhesive tape holding his glasses together and never considered how it might look.

He's always been too concerned with defensing the four-corner delay to worry about such things. His reputation, though, was different. That's why the last two seasons have been so long; he's had two straight losing seasons at Northwestern. That's not unusual for Northwestern, but it is for Tex Winter.

"It's hard to get used to losing" he said at the NCAA tournament. "I'm a little jealous of my image and reputation. I've spent a lot of time building a good reputation."

That he has. This is his 22nd year in college basketball and he's had some great ones. The best, no doubt, were at Kansas State where he won eight Big Eight titles in 15 years and finished one season ranked No. 1 in the country.

He's never had success quite like that since. Part of that is Tex's own doing. You see, Winter wants only to coach intelligent players. He refused when he was at Kansas State, to take just anybody who could hit the 20-foot jumper. And he won that way.

"But one of the reasons I left," he said, "was that the competition in the Big Eight had reached the point where I thought I would have to take a whole lot of athletes that I didn't want to take—the marginal students."

That's why he liked Northwestern. It's a school of just 8,000 students and most everyone there can give you the square root of 149 to the fourth decimal point without hesitation.

Not many high school basketball players can do that. That limits Winter's recruiting considerably. You have to wonder if Winter can make it under those circumstances.

"It depends on what you consider making it," he said. "I think we can be a contender on occasional seasons, win the conference maybe every once in a while. Playing .500 ball there is about the best you can hope for.

"There are just so many more academic restrictions. I don't care how good of an athlete you are, if you're not in the top 10 in the class you don't have a ghost of a chance of getting in."

That, he concedes, is the kind of situation he likes. But he also likes winning.

"The big adjustment I have to make is being happy playing .500 ball," he said. "If I can, then I'll be all right."

"It's just that I hate to see my record go down—particularly in the twilight of my career."

Winter probably would make Northwestern his last job—he's in his mid-50s—if he could win there.

Wichita Eagle March 31, 1975

Tex says

Northwestern coaching was a good job for me. For one thing, I couldn't waste a lot of time recruiting. There were only one or two Chicago All-City team members during those five years who would even qualify at Northwestern, because the standards were so high. We played teams in the Big Ten tough, but we just couldn't win a lot of close games. We did beat Michigan when they were rated #1 in the nation, and we beat the University of Iowa who was rated high. We also beat Minnesota when they were nationally ranked. We played Indiana really well in a couple of games but didn't win. That's kind of the way it went.

Krause and Tex first met when Krause came to Kansas State games, scouting for the Baltimore Bullets. Tex befriended him, spent time talking basketball, and they watched 16mm films of many games. Krause wanted to know everything about Tex's triple post offense. He had stayed in touch with Tex ever since. "When I get an NBA general manager job," Krause said. "I want you to come and help me."

"Sure, Jerry," Tex replied and left it at that.

Tex's five-year record at Northwestern University was 44 wins and 87 losses, but he didn't base his success on the record only.▲ He intended to develop players, and he had done that. "It was a good, interesting job," Tex told colleagues about his experience, "but I am now ranked fourteenth as a winning college coach. I don't want to go down any farther. I would like to have an equal opportunity to win."

Northwestern University Varsity 1976–77

Back Row: Assistant Rich Falk, David Fields, Mike Campbell, Bob Klaas, Chris Wall, (unidentified), Manager Jim Reinert.

Middle Row: Coach Winter, Randy Carroll, Brad Cartwright, Bob Svete, Pete Boesen, David Hiser, Tony Allen, Manager John Caccese.

Front Row: Assistant Walt Perrin, Brian Gibson, Jim Endsley, Billy McKinney, Bob Hildebrand, Jerry Marifke, Bill Fenlon.

Long Beach State Varsity 1978-79

Back Row: Manager Gerry Grandusky, Phil Gary, Craig Lack, Craig Dykema, Michael Wiley, Jeff Fagan, Kevin Tye, Francoise Wise, Kelly Johnson, Mose Braziel, Trainer Dan Bailey.

Middle Row: Manager Doug Heitman, Manager Rick Lamprecht, Dave Shutts, Chuck Cowlings, Ray Reeves, Crawford Richmond, Craig Hodges, Steve Hair, Ron Mason, Doug Ferguson, Assistant Coach Lauren Proctor.

Front Row: Assistant Coach Dan Carnevale, Coach Winter, Assistant Coach Jerry Chandler.

49ers Hire Winter as Coach

Coming off an unsuccessful stint at Northwestern, veteran basketball coach Tex Winter was named the new head man at Long Beach State Thursday.

The former college coach of the year at Kansas State and tutor of the Houston Rockets of the NBA ranks ninth in the nation among major college coaches in career victories with 374 compared to 266 despite a 44–87 record in five years at Northwestern.

Winter called the Long Beach opportunity "excellent for me personally. I hope we can continue the tradition of Long Beach basketball but it is something I can't do alone. We'll need dedication from the returning players and those we recruit."

Orange County Register April 7, 1978

In the spring of 1978, Tex traveled to Southern California on a recruiting trip for Northwestern. While there, he was contacted by the athletic director, Perry Moore, at California State University, Long Beach (Long Beach State).

Long Beach State enjoyed a winning tradition, but had been sanctioned by the NCAA. They also had a problem attracting good teams to play. With Tex's history, the athletic director thought Tex could help. "We want you to be our head basketball coach," he told Tex.

Tex hadn't intended to leave Northwestern, but he and Nancy would be closer to family if they returned to California. He also thought he would have a chance to increase his personal "college games won" ranking. Tex became Long Beach State's basketball coach.

The school had been put on four-year probation. Tex also had been chosen over another coach who was favored by players, fans, and the press.

Tex pushed ahead. His Long Beach 49ers won their first eight games against tough competitors, including Kansas State. Fans gave the young team good support.

Soon Tex discovered some players had been promised additional money. They transferred when Tex did not continue the "extra" payments they demanded. Tex also learned that some competitor schools had recruited players with illegal gifts and favors.

Tex retained the existing assistant coaches, but after a couple of years, Long Beach's administration assigned a former Long Beach State All-America player as an assistant coach without checking with Tex first.

Long Beach State's small gymnasium did not accommodate the large crowd of fans that began following the team. Games were moved to the downtown arena. But that venue had its share of problems too. One local reporter described it as a disgrace to the city with its inadequate parking, unacceptable lighting, and ceiling tiles either missing or badly stained.

"Attitudes of all his players were always very important to Tex, and he would remind us that we were in the public eye. He always told us that he did not want any 'prima donnas'."

Nick Pino
Kansas State University 1968

Tex says

I've always been particular about who I associate with and how I live my life. When I decided to become a coach, I started preparing myself to be an example for young men. I don't tolerate bad attitudes or bad habits in myself. I don't tolerate them in others very well either.

Each year brought new difficulties until a season of nearly equal wins and losses did not please fans. Dissatisfaction built.

That wasn't all. A group of heckling fans made themselves at home directly behind the Long Beach State bench. With paper bags over their heads, they harassed Tex and his players during a couple of home games. They wanted a fast-paced run-and-shoot game instead of the organized, controlled play using Tex's Triangle.

With all these problems threatening the entire program, Tex wondered if Long Beach State's basketball program would survive, with or without him. ▲

Tex and Dan Carnevale, assistant coach, direct their LBS 49ers courtside.

Tex stayed at Long Beach for five years with a record of 85 wins and 69 losses. All in all, it was a good experience, Tex reported, but he was tired. Rumors about his retirement were whispered here and there, some of which he started himself.

In spite of all the problems at Long Beach State, Tex was honored by his peers and elected president of the National Association of Basketball Coaches for 1983. The annual convention, in conjunction with the NCAA Final Four tournament, was in Albuquerque, New Mexico. Tex presided.

Louisiana State University 1984–85. Back Row: Assistant Bo Bahnsen, Assistant Johnny Jones, Head Coach Dale Brown, Jose Vargas, Damon Vance, Zoran Jovanovich, Jerry Reynolds, John Williams, Assistant Coach Ron Abernathy, Assistant Coach Tex Winter, Trainer Dr. Marty Broussard. Front Row: Ricky Blanton, Ollie Brown, Nikita Wilson, Ocie Conley, Derrick Taylor, Dennis Brown, Neboisha Bukumirovich, Anthony Wilson, Don Redden.

Tex says

Dale was a coach from a North Dakota high school who had read my book, *The Triple Post Offense*. He called and said he'd like to spend a week with me. He followed me around to practices and games. He wanted to use the Triangle with his teams. He did, and he had good teams. He became head coach at Louisiana State University.

In his book *Tiger in a Lion's Den*, Dale listed me as one of the seven most respected men in his life. "Perhaps the most special trait of Tex Winter is his unselfishness," he wrote.

"When I was a high school coach in North Dakota and Tex was coaching at Kansas State, I wrote him a letter. He was hot; everyone in the country wanted him. He was coach of the year. His team was in the Final Four and ranked number one in the nation. I told him I wanted to come and learn basketball from him. He took me to his home, took me to the country club, stayed up late at night, watched multitudes of films, and talked to me one-on-one. He treated a no-name guy with great dignity. I was so impressed with how genuine and down-to-earth he was."

Dale Brown

Dale Brown
Dale Brown Enterprises

86

Dale Brown, head basketball coach at Louisiana State University, warmly greeted Tex in Albuquerque. They had met at Kansas State where they had spent hours talking about the Triangle offense and studying 16mm films.▲

Coach Brown deplored Tex's experience at Long Beach State. "You're too good to be treated that way," Brown told Tex. "Why don't you come work with me for a couple of years? I want you to help me coach and teach."

The offer sounded good to Tex. He became Brown's consultant, teaching team fundamentals and coaching players individually.

Using the Triangle, the two coaches built a great record, won a Southeast Conference Championship, and advanced to the NCAA playoffs. "Everyone loves Tex," Coach Brown told his administrators. "He's a great teacher and coach—honest with no frills."

Tex had been at LSU two seasons when he again heard about Jerry Krause. "Krause got the GM job with the Bulls," Tex told Nancy. "The next time the phone rings, it will be Jerry."

Nancy said she wouldn't mind returning to the Chicago area. She had enjoyed living there when Tex coached at Northwestern, and she was ready to leave Louisiana behind.

Tex says

I picked up the phone. "Well, I got the Chicago Bulls general manager job," Krause said. "You have to come and help me."

Tex and Nancy Winter

"No, Jerry. I'm retiring, and Nancy and I are on our way to Salem, Oregon," I told him. "We bought a retirement home, and we like it very much. I appreciate your thinking of me."

"You promised me."

"I never made any promises."

"Oh, yes you did."

"Well, Jerry, make it worth my while."

Krause offered me $60,000 to join the Bulls.

"No, Jerry. No, no, that won't do it." I replied.

But I was tempted. The pro basketball picture had changed since my days with the Rockets. Maybe these high level players could be taught the Triangle, like Jerry wanted. Besides, the most I'd ever made was $36,000 per year as a college coach.

"How about $75,000?"

"Okay, I'll be there."

Offensive Build-Up Drills

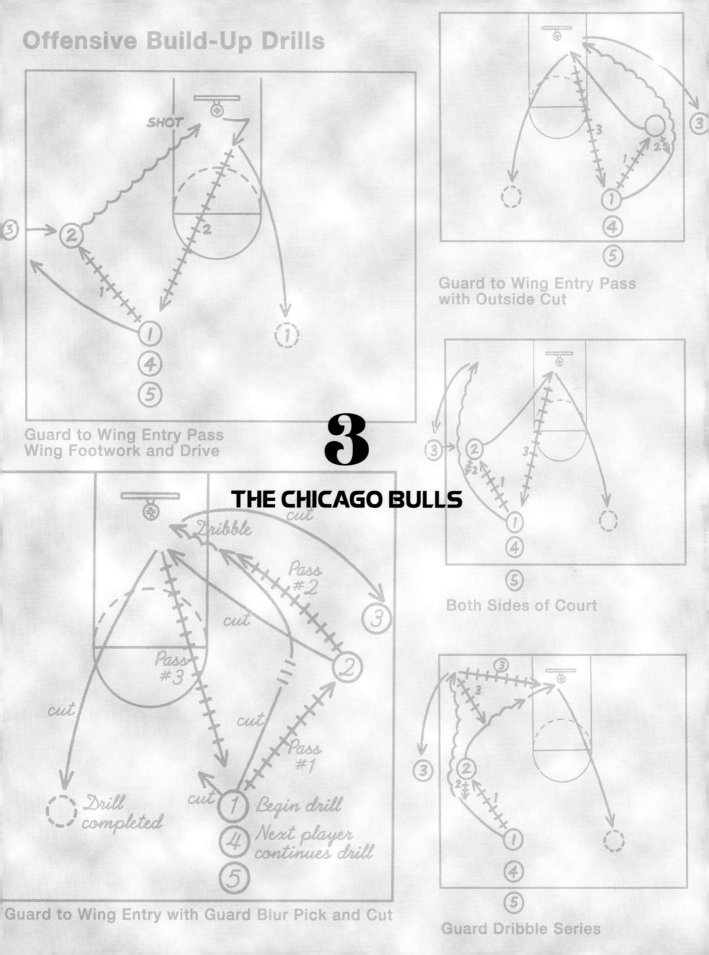

Guard to Wing Entry Pass Wing Footwork and Drive

Guard to Wing Entry Pass with Outside Cut

Both Sides of Court

3

THE CHICAGO BULLS

Guard to Wing Entry with Guard Blur Pick and Cut

Guard Dribble Series

State Ka
Sports Hall of
TEX WIN
Inducte Jul

cut

Pass #2

Pass #1

Begin drill

Next player continues drill

Michael Jordan skipped his senior year at the University of North Carolina to play professional basketball.

Tex's new employer, the Chicago Bulls professional basketball team, had finished their twentieth season in 1984 with twice as many losses as wins. Management scratched their heads. How could they jump-start the team?

The year before, they had chosen a player named Michael Jordan from the University of North Carolina as the third pick in the NBA draft.

Tex says

It was the 1983 NBA draft. Time for making choices from the list of picks. The Houston Rockets where I had coached earlier, chose Hakeem Olajuwon, the expected first choice. He was an outstanding player. That left Sam Bowie and Michael Jordan. The Portland Trailblazers, with second pick, took Sam Bowie. Bowie was a big guy, but he had bad legs. We played against him at LSU when he was at the University of Kentucky. He was a good player, big player, about 7'2", but he still wouldn't have been a better pick than Michael Jordan. That left Michael for the Chicago Bulls. I always thought the Trailblazers must have scratched their heads for a long time, wondering why they chose Bowie over Michael.

I knew Michael was unafraid to act when a game was on the line. I especially admired that he dared to take UNC's game-winning shot against Georgetown in the 1982 national championship final. That impressed me. Lucky for us, because he understood the necessity of working as a team after playing under coaches Dean Smith and my former player, Bill Guthridge, assistant coach, at North Carolina.

Tex says

During the preseason camp, Michael stood out. He had exceptional reflexes and outstanding vision. I noticed how he could anticipate players next moves. He instinctively challenged, intercepted, or moved into the passing lane whenever an opponent telegraphed a pass. I teased the other coaches that the only person who had kept Michael below an eighteen-point-per-game average was his college coach, Dean Smith. And of course, that was because Michael had been brought up with the idea of team play.

Tex grabs a quiet moment to think about ways to help the team.

Tex had seen Jordan play at UNC against LSU. He noticed his competitiveness. He thought Jordan showed a deep understanding of the game. Tex saw his quickness, his jumping ability, and the many different ways he moved to the basket. But as good as Jordan was, Tex picked out areas that, when strengthened, would make Jordan an even better player.▲

The next season, Tex's first with the Bulls, Jordan scored forty-nine points against the Boston Celtics in a first-round playoff game; the Bulls lost. He scored sixty-three points in the second game with the Celtics; the Bulls lost again.

Tex saw the predicament: how to blend Jordan's unique talents into a team setting. Jordan was a great player. But how could his high scoring help the team?▲ Something had to change. The Bulls's head coach, Stan Albeck, might not have been the problem, but Jerry Krause fired him anyway.

> *Never be satisfied with your present development.*

Tex says

Before going into the off-season Los Angeles summer league that I coached, Jerry Krause and I talked. We agreed that Phil Jackson would be my assistant. It was a way to introduce Phil to my philosophy of basketball. Phil watched as I broke down drills to teach the principles and run plays. Phil said the way I coached was a method of basketball that he wanted to hold on to, similar to what he played with the New York Knicks. That was fortunate for me. Phil recognized the advantage of the Triangle approach and how you can teach it to players. If Phil had not taken to the Triangle, I might have been out of the game for good.

"Tex is a born leader. Players take to him with respect. Many times during games he made key substitutions or time-outs, dictating our offense and defense that changed the course of the game. He had the ability to notice things that most coaches could not."

Grant Wittberger, Marquette University 1953

Tex and Phil Jackson begin a long-lasting partnership.

94

Jerry Krause went looking for a head coach who would use Tex's Triangle. Instead, when Coach Doug Collins took over, he gave Jordan all the time and space he wanted on the court.

Tex could have predicted the outcome. Jordan dominated games, scoring sixty points twice, fifty or more in three straight games, and the Bulls still lost. Jordan's teammates often looked like stage props, standing around, watching Jordan wear himself out. Tex didn't think Jordan was making the contribution Tex knew he could and wanted to. Tex wondered if the Triangle would ever be part of the Bulls's playing strategy. Tex was ready to quit.

New players were brought in to help Jordan, and Phil Jackson was hired as an assistant coach. Tex and Jackson talked, recalling the days Jackson had played for Red Holzman with the New York Knicks who won the NBA title in 1972. "Your Knicks team played with a lot of savvy," Tex told Jackson. "You had a bunch of stars, very intelligent guys."

Tex recognized similarities between the Triangle and the team approach that Holzman had used. As Tex described the Triangle offense and demonstrated how it worked, Jackson showed keen interest. ▲

The next season, 1987-88, did not go well either. Jordan didn't care for the new line-up of players. Coach Collins's offense plan fizzled. The Bulls lost to the Detroit Pistons in the end-of-season playoffs. Coach Collins was fired.

Michael Jordan attempts to settle Doug Collins, center, while assistant coaches Tex, right, and Johnny Bach, left look on.

"Tex was a demanding coach and he expected improvement on the court. But he was equally interested, and perhaps more so, in helping his players grow as human beings to prepare for the great game of life."

Bob VanVooren
Bob VanVooren
Marquette University
1955

Phil Jackson, now head coach of the Bulls, joins forces with Tex to work with Michael Jordan.

Michael interpreted our early efforts as the "de-Michaelization" of the Bulls. "Players today can do things they couldn't twenty years ago," Michael complained. "The game isn't played like Tex Winter or Phil Jackson taught it. Those concepts don't work against bigger, faster players who jump higher...players who create."

Tex says

More Than a Game

By Phil Jackson and Charley Rosen.

Basketball is a game of moment-to-moment action, and this is where I'm able to bring Zen into the picture. Practicing any kind of Zen or Buddhist meditation (which I do) is attempting to bring yourself back to the moment. One breath to the next breath.

As you meditate, all kinds of thoughts are going to come pouring into your mind. You've got to go to the dentist that afternoon. The rent bill is due today. What did your friend mean yesterday when she said...? But you stay focused on your breath because the breath is the only thing that's real and present in the moment, while your thoughts are just biochemical energy flashing around inside your brain that have no inherent reality.

In basketball it's playing one play, then playing the next play. If you're thinking about how long it's been since you took a shot, or what move you're going to make the next time the ball comes to you, or how that last foul on you was such a bad call, then your mind gets in the way of the game.

Players learn to love the game when they can get into the moment, the here and now, and lose themselves in it. Suddenly they're just breathing and playing basketball and it's all natural and it's all exactly what it's supposed to be. There's no conflict with their teammates, and the door's wide open in front of them.

New York: Seven Stories Press, 2001.

Labels in diagram: cut, Dribble, Pass #2, cut, 3, 2, cut, Pass #1, 1 Begin drill, 4 Next player continues drill, 5, Drill completed, cut

---

Phil Jackson became head coach. He wanted to implement the Triangle. He asked Tex to be his assistant coach as offense coordinator. Tex agreed.

Jordan would be shown how the Triangle could help, how it would make him an even greater player, and how his teammates could contribute. Most important was convincing Jordan that this improvement could happen when he didn't have possession of the ball.▲ Tex and Jackson wanted him to involve his teammates more.

Tex and Jackson talked to Jordan about the Triangle. Jordan hesitated. The coaches kept talking. Jordan wanted evidence that coaches and teammates were committed to the plan. Jordan agreed to try it.

Michael Jordan Retirement Comments

From Michael Jordan's comments during his retirement news conference:

Question: Michael, which were you more proud of, your athletic skills or the mental skills that you brought to the game, and which was more difficult to keep up?

Michael: Well, I came in here with the physical skills. To some degree I was born with the appetite to enhance it as I got older and as I played the game. But the mental skills came with the education of the game that I learned either from Coach Smith before I got here or I learned in the course of the coaching staffs that I have been endeared with, Tex Winter probably being the most, because he was probably the one that would criticize my game more than anybody. To me that's a plus, that's a driving force for me. The mental part is hard because you have to really learn, taking everything that you've learned over a period of time, and apply that to your game and tie that into the physical aspect of your game and make the complete basketball player that you try to become. So physically, it's a little bit easier, but the mental part is the hardest part, and I think that's the part that separates the good players from the great players.

http://sportsillustrated.cnn.com
August 8, 2001

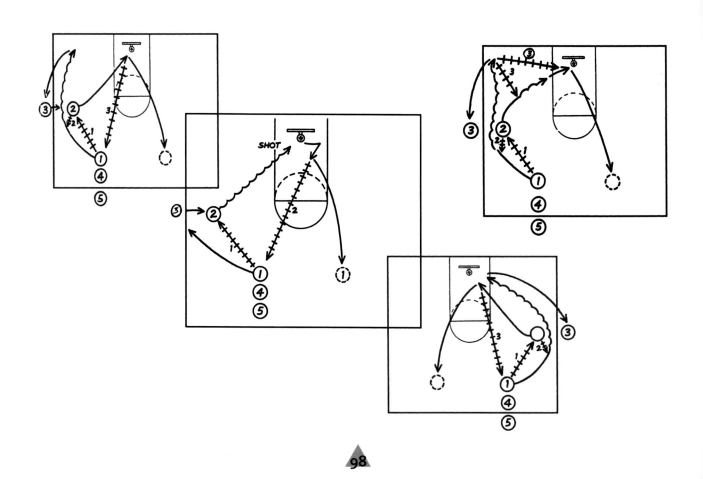

Jordan practiced the Triangle with his teammates. He had
agreed to give the Triangle serious effort, and he did. The team
worked hard, building their skills and developing trust in each
other. Jordan's performance did not diminish. In fact, during a
late season game, he scored a career high of sixty-nine points.
The Bulls prepared to face the Detroit Pistons, defending NBA
champions, for the second time in the 1989 Eastern Conference
finals.

But Jordan slipped into old habits. Several of his teammates
were injured, but so was he. He expected them to come through
as he did. When they didn't, he felt abandoned. He tried to beat
the Pistons by himself. This new team strategy—the Triangle—
was supposed to spread the load around. In his opinion, it didn't
work. Tex, frustrated, shook his head.

#1 Prejudice is a great time saver. It enables you to form opinions without bothering to get the facts.

#2 The reason girls would rather be good looking than smart is because boys can see a lot better than they can think.

#3 A liberal education to many students these days seems to mean a generous allowance.

#4 When you sing your own praises you may sound out of tune to your listeners.

"Tex could be impatient, since he was, and probably still is, a perfectionist. Plays had to be run with precision, crispness, and understanding of what was going on. You couldn't bluff your way through practice, or if he asked you what you were supposed to be doing on a play and you didn't know, there was no faking it."

Steve Hawes
University of Washington 1972

During the next season, Jordan was given free rein to shoot the ball, and that tactic worked to a point. But the Pistons again outdid the Bulls for the championship. *Basketball is a team sport*, Tex reminded himself. *Everybody brings something, and to win consistently, you have to be hitting on all cylinders. We aren't doing that.*

Could he and Jackson, once and for all, persuade Jordan to give the Triangle his whole effort? Or would Jordan, like the Navy Lieutenant Commander years earlier, turn and walk off?

"Michael," Jackson said, "we've got to get some of the pressure off you."

Tex knew Jackson was referring to the Pistons's "Jordan Rules," a plan the Pistons had concocted to stop Jordan. One Piston player would forearm Jordan as he drove past while the next player was in position to bump or push Jordan. Pistons players would grab players at pressure points to deaden their arms. Jordan was their first target. When Jordan tried to do too much, he fell victim to their plan, and ended up getting hurt.

Jordan returned for the 1990-91 season, ready to do what was necessary to beat the Pistons.

Pass
#2

3

2

Pass
#1

1 Begin drill

4 Next player
continues drill

5

Tex, right, and
Phil Jackson track
the action.

Tex watches the action, analyzing each move to provide feedback and make suggestions.

Winter comfortable as Bulls's assistant

By Bob Hentzen

Tex Winter wears a ring commemorating his term as president of the National Basketball Coaches Association. Soon, he will have a fancy new ring—an NBA championship ring.

Winter has been a member of the Bulls's staff for six seasons, under three head coaches. He has remained because of his relationship with Jerry Krause, the general manager.

"I've known him since he graduated from Bradley," Winter related. "When I was at Northwestern, he was a scout for the Bulls and came to lunch every week. He said if he ever became a general manager he wanted to have me.

"He brought me in initially—I don't want to sound conceited—to tutor, be the mentor, for the head coach. I'm sort of a coach of coaches. I outline what we ought to be doing."

Winter admits that there always wasn't a lot of job satisfaction when he was working for Stan Albeck and then Doug Collins. But that's changed with Jackson.

"He's easy to work for," he said. "I feel like I've made a valuable contribution since Jackson took over. Before that I was frustrated. I didn't feel like I was contributing."

Jackson turns the first 30 minutes of every practice over to Winter.

"We do fundamental drills," Winter said. "Believe it or not, we do the same drills we did at K-State 30 years ago."

The Bulls's offense now also has Winter's stamp. They basically run the "triple-post" that he put together at Kansas Sate.

"Of course, we do some other things," he said. "But it is very gratifying to see Michael Jordan accept that philosophy. It's a team concept and takes away from one-on-one type of play. But he learned to love it. It's why we got so tough at the end of the year."

The Topeka Capital-Journal, Sunday, September 22, 1991

Jordan still wasn't sure the Triangle was the answer.

Tex reminded Jordan that it wouldn't be easy, that it would take time. "Will you give it your best?" Tex asked.

Jordan finally agreed.

That season, the Bulls finished with the best shooting average in their history, fifty-one percent. They were ready for their biggest enemy—the Detroit Pistons.

Toward the end of Game One in the conference playoffs, the Bulls led the Pistons by three points. Tex told Jackson he ought to shake things up a bit, keep the players alert, and make them pay close attention. Jackson agreed. He called the starters, including Jordan, to the bench. He put the second team on the floor. "Man, what are you doing?" Tex asked.

Tex knew that the second team often stayed with the Triangle in a more disciplined way, but he feared Jackson's move might have been too much of a shake-up.

In less than six minutes, the second team had built up a nine-point lead.

"That move took guts," Tex told Jackson. "Your timing was right. They did a great job." More evidence of the powerful partnership between Coaches Winter and Jackson.

Michael Jordan flies high with Pistons
player James Edwards.

The Bulls won the 1991 Eastern Finals in four games straight. Finally, the Bulls under Jackson's expert leadership and Tex's wise counsel, had turned things around and gained a victory over the Pistons. They were ready to meet the Los Angeles Lakers for the NBA finals, looking for their first-ever national championship.

Using the Triangle and an aggressive, man-to-man full-court pressing defense, the Chicago Bulls beat the Los Angeles Lakers in five games and won their first NBA championship. Jordan and Scottie Pippen and Bill Cartwright were tough on defense. They are naturals, Tex concluded. He watched as Cartwright often reduced high scoring centers to about half their scoring average.

Tex's Xs and Os had walked off his clipboard and danced themselves all around the court like a five-sided dazzling pyramid. Tex had known this would happen. Now everyone else had seen it with their own eyes.

The Bulls won their first three championships in the old Chicago arena before the United Center was built across the street. Known as "The Madhouse on Madison," the Chicago Stadium was home to the Chicago Bulls from 1968 to 1994. It was demolished in 1995. The center circle from the Chicago Bulls's floor is in Michael Jordan's trophy room in his house.

Sacred Hoops

by Phil Jackson and Hugh Delehanty

Introduction

When I was named head coach of the Chicago Bulls in 1989, my dream was not just to win championships, but to do it in a way that wove together my two greatest passions: basketball and spiritual exploration.

The day I took over the Bulls, I vowed to create an environment based on the principles of selflessness and compassion I'd learned as a Christian in my parents' home; sitting on a cushion practicing Zen; and studying the teachings of the Lakota Sioux. I knew that the only way to win consistently was to give everybody—from the stars to the number 12 player on the bench—a vital role on the team, and inspire them to be acutely aware of what was happening, even when the spotlight was on somebody else. More than anything, I wanted to build a team that would blend individual talent with a heightened group consciousness. A team that could win big without becoming small in the process.

The more I learned about the Bulls, the more intrigued I became. The coaching staff included a couple of the best minds in the game: Johnny Bach, a man with an encyclopedic knowledge of basketball, and Tex Winter, the innovator of the famed triangle offense, a system that emphasizes cooperation and freedom, the very values I'd spent my life pursuing off the court and dreamed of applying to the game.

This isn't always an easy task in a society where the celebration of ego is the number one national pastime. Nowhere is this more true than in the hothouse atmosphere of professional sports. Yet even in this highly competitive world, I've discovered that when you free players to use all their resources—mental, physical, and spiritual—an interesting shift in awareness occurs. When players practice what is known as mindfulness—simply paying attention to what's actually happening—not only do they play better and win more, they also become more attuned with each other. And the joy they experience working in harmony is a powerful motivating force that comes from deep within, not from some frenzied coach pacing along the sidelines, shouting obscenities into the air.

A Tribute to the 1991 NBA Champion Chicago Bulls

It was a crowded flight the Chicago Bulls boarded at the beginning of the NBA season, for expectations and aspirations can make for uncomfortable companions.

After all, the Bulls had been to the Eastern Conference finals twice. They had the game's most exciting player in Michael "Air" Jordan and the heir apparent in high flying Scottie Pippen. Their rookies had gotten some experience, and they had added some veterans. It was time.

They won more games than any team in franchise history in their silver anniversary season. But they were golden after the All-Star break in compiling the league's best record, as they won 20 of 21 in one stretch and 26 straight at home.

They led the late news in highlight film clips, but they ultimately did it with defense. They were first in flight with Jordan and first in might with an aggressive, rapping, pressured, bumping, thumping, belly-to-belly defense masterminded by coaches Phil Jackson and John Bach that sent opponents crashing and burning. They stole your hearts and wore down your soles.

Sure, there was some turbulence along the way. They bounced through some contract hassles and youthful frustrations. And they had to answer the critics, who said you don't win with the league's leading scorer, that you don't win with one man. But they never let their hands stray from the controls. And when they were in final approach, it was glorious. They glided and then struck with precision in the league finals. Their shots were heard 'round the world while their defense caused tremors. And the NBA's earth moved.

For the first time, the Bulls and Air Jordan soared to the top of the NBA.

Sam Smith

Chicago Tribune

Wheaties, 1991

Pictures on 107

Left
Back row:
Coach Jim Cleamons,
Coach Tex Winter,
Head Coach Phil Jackson,
Coach John Bach,
Trainer Chip Schaefer.
Middle row:
Craig Hodges,
Cliff Levingston,
Scott Williams,
Will Perdue,
Stacey King,
Dennis Hopson.
Front row:
John Paxson,
Horace Grant,
Bill Cartwright,
Scottie Pippen,
Michael Jordan,
B.J. Armstrong.

Right
John Paxson,
Scottie Pippen,
B.J. Armstrong.
Michael Jordan,
Horace Grant,
Bill Cartwright.

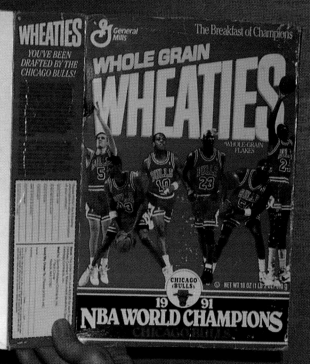

Chicago Bulls player #24, Bill Cartwright, sets to score against the Blazers.

Tex says

That was an amazing thing to watch. Phil shaking things up. That really turned things around for us. After the second team got going, I didn't even want Phil to put the starters back in, but he finally did. That was probably a good thing. Proved that staying with the Triangle system really works. Fortunately, the second team had open shots, and they hit them. That was really fun to watch.

Michael Jordan, #23, soars over the Blazers to reach for Championship #2.

cu

#1

Begin drill

Next player continues drill

The Bulls earned their way to the 1992 finals too and played the Portland Trailblazers for the championship. In the last game of the series, the Bulls trailed by seventeen points at the half. Tex eyed the basketball floor. Yes, the starters had come to the game. But they didn't look like they were ready to play, let alone fight for their second title. In fact, they looked as if they hardly had shown up at all. Tex leaned over and said to Jackson. "Coach, we've gotta do something. Shake things up."

Again, Jackson pulled the starters from the game, lined up second team players, and sent them to the floor. Tex remembered the same move one season earlier, but this time it wasn't a conference finals game. It was for the championship title. ▲

Because those bench-warmers were ready to execute the Triangle, the Bulls won their second NBA title, final game score 97-91.

Fans were overjoyed when the Bulls had won their first-ever title the year before against the Los Angeles Lakers. Now, with a second championship to celebrate, they refused to leave the

"Tex as an outstanding 'teacher' of the game of basketball. His teams were always fundamentally sound. Maybe this is why: he was one of the first to break down his offense so that everyday fundamental practice drills were part of the offense."

Dean Plagge
Kansas State University 1958

Bulls, Jordan borrow from K-State

By Mal Elliott

Kansas State basketball fans probably noticed something familiar. The Bulls's triangle offense.

Winter wrote the book on the offense. He wrote it in 1962, the year before Jordan was born. It was called the triple post offense. It was Kansas State's offense then, the same offense Winter used to win eight Big Eight Conference titles between 1953 and 1968.

In 1989, Jackson was named head coach of the Bulls, and he made Winter his offensive coordinator.

The rest is history.

"He was looking for an offense that involved five players," Winter said. "He just adapted it wholeheartedly. I might leave a bit of a legacy here. That pleases me very much."

Winter said the triple post involves a lot of elements of the old Drake shuffle, created by Oklahoma University's Hall of Fame coach Bruce Drake. It's a continuity offense; the longer you run it, the more scoring options open up. In the NBA, however, you only have 24 seconds. "So it has to be quick-hitting," Winter said.

The triple post is driving other NBA teams nuts.

"Most pro teams go to pro sets," Winter said. "They have set plays, and they call them and run them.

"We don't call plays. Everything is keyed off player position and ball movement. I think it's caused considerable consternation because they're not used to that. It's predicated on countering the defense."

In other words, it takes what the defense gives. And if you've watched much pro basketball, you may have noticed the defense is sometimes inclined to give away the farm.

"The first year we ran it (1989-90), we didn't win the championship. Detroit beat us out," Winter said. "It was an adjustment period for these pro players. Especially Michael Jordan, who was playing isolation-type basketball."

The next season, though, the Bulls won their division and beat the Lakers in five games for the NBA title. They repeated last season, putting together the NBA's best record and then beating Portland in six games for the championship.

"These pro players have such talents; it's not Michael who needs it, or Scottie Pippen," Winter said of the triple post. "It's the other guys. You need to get all five players involved in the offense.

"It's to Michael's and Pippen's credit that they saw that. They saw the objectives and reason behind it, and it became more effective. We saw a real change come over the team.

"Jordan is still leading the league in scoring with 32 points a game and doing it so much easier. He's not taking the beating he took to get those 32 points. I think it's going to prolong his career."

The Wichita Eagle,
Sunday, August 9, 1992

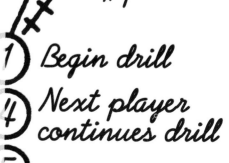

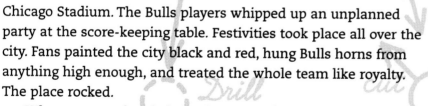

Chicago Stadium. The Bulls players whipped up an unplanned party at the score-keeping table. Festivities took place all over the city. Fans painted the city black and red, hung Bulls horns from anything high enough, and treated the whole team like royalty. The place rocked.

When congratulated about the game, Tex said, "Yeah, we won, but look how we played."

Most did not welcome his comments. Especially his wife Nancy, who said, "You ought to quit coaching. You don't get any joy out of it any more."

"It's how you play the game," Tex retorted, "not whether you win or lose. Besides, think of all the people that watched us play so badly on television."

"And what about the millions in China who didn't see you?" she asked. Tex cooled a bit.

"I guess it is about whether you win or lose," Tex said, thinking he had already finished the conversation. "But I've always preached the fundamentals to players and coaches. Drill the fundamentals and you will play well."

The Bulls had not played well, and he was not pleased.

Pass #1

1 Begin drill

4 Next player continues drill

5 Tex catches up on box scores in the locker room corner.

Michael Jordan and his father, James, share a moment with the media.

Tex says

I saw Michael sitting in the visitors locker room with his greatest supporter, his father James, to his right. James watched as Michael cried tears of joy, tears of satisfaction, tears of fulfillment. "I'm numb," Michael said between sobs. "I don't know what to do. I want to enjoy this, it's such a great feeling. We took it, and we took it as a team. That's what I'm proudest about. I played my game, but with the efforts everybody gave, we did it as a team."

I calmly smiled, giving away my pure pleasure at the pulling together of six years of hard work. Phil had done a masterful job of incorporating Michael's exceptional talent into a team effort without weakening his play. Now I knew you could win in the NBA without a dominant center. You could win with a leading-scorer guard. But I knew most of all you have to have a fully functioning team.

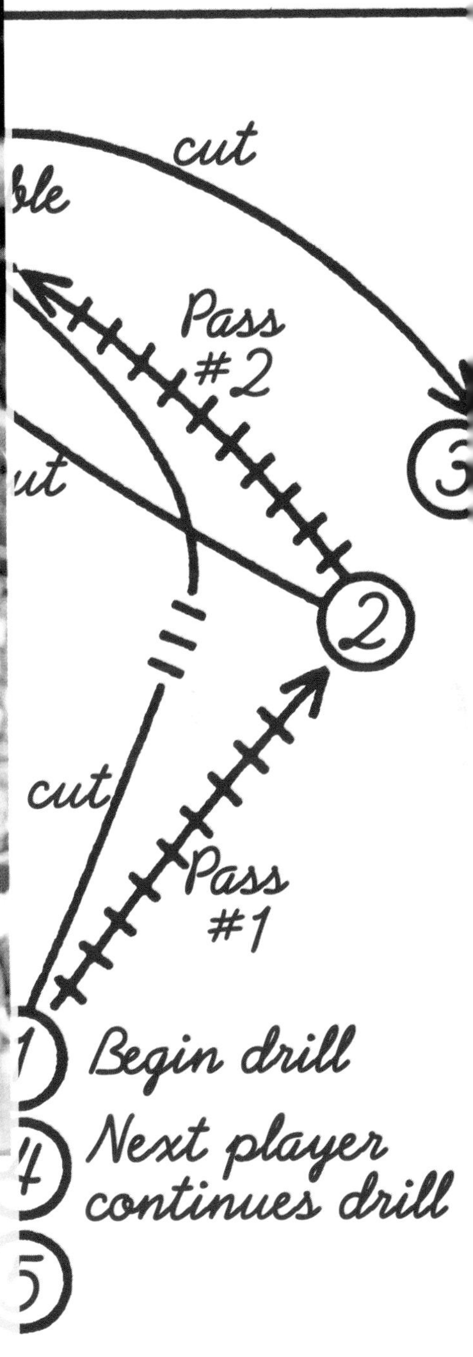

cut

ble

Pass #2

ut

③

②

cut

Pass #1

① Begin drill

④ Next player continues drill

⑤

Horace Grant, #54, does his part to score in spite of Phoenix Suns Charles Barkley's effort.

With two championships earned, the Bulls moved into the 1992-93 season. Tex and Jackson welcomed the challenge to make history by winning their third NBA title in a row. The players welcomed the possibility too. By the end of the season, the Bulls were playing the Phoenix Suns for the title.

The Suns won only once by forcing the third game into a triple overtime. But in the last game, the Bulls went cold. Behind by two points with only fourteen seconds left, Tex watched closely as Jackson drew up a play for Jordan to take the final shot. Instead, Jordan passed the ball to Scottie Pippen, who passed to Horace Grant, who passed to John Paxson, who shot the winning three-point basket. Victory. A third title.▲

> "One of the reasons Tex has been able to stay at coaching so long is his ability to not get 'too high' with a win or 'too low' with a loss."

Bill Guthridge
Kansas State University 1960

April 22, 1995

Sports Editor Roy Gault

You would think that after four decades in coaching, Winter would have seen and done everything. But it was then that he won his first championship.

"The first one was quite a thrill," he said. "It came kind of unexpected. The second one was more of a relief. The third was a Godsend."

So, Tex Winter finally has accomplished virtually all there is to accomplish in basketball.

Salem Statesman Journal
Salem, Oregon

Tex says

Because Phil liked my Triangle ideas, I have had a job for many years. I tried to retire several times, but Phil's use of the Triangle keeps me going. I think he values what I have to say about how the team is doing. He counts on my observations about players, and he counts on the individual work I do with players. We have a good working relationship. He seems to respect my wisdom, and I respect his ability to stay calm and trust his players in most any circumstance.

114

"Tex has the charisma that makes him instantly likeable and believable. I was impressed with his down-to-earth approach and honesty when he recruited me in 1962. Even with the fame and recognition he's received through the years, his honesty and sincerity are still two of his greatest traits today. He's had a tremendous influence on my life."

Larry Weigel

Larry Weigel

Kansas State University 1968

Tex didn't complain about how they played this time. Even the last play, the critical game-winning shot, showcased the Triangle's best features. Every player was alert, ready to make a pass or shoot a basket. When the defense went one way, Jordan and his teammates went the other. "That play was how we wanted our offense to work all year," Tex said to fans who congratulated him. "Michael's going to create the play, even if he doesn't take the shot."

Tex had dreamed about teamwork like that fifty-six years earlier, sitting on a bench at Huntington Park High School, watching Loyola college players form triangles. Now he was coaching the nation's finest professional players, fine-tuning the Triangle, watching its execution help win world championships. ▲

Jury convicts 21-year-old in murder of Jordan's father

February 29, 1996

LUMBERTON, North Carolina—After deliberating almost five hours, a jury Thursday convicted a 21-year-old man of murdering basketball star Michael Jordan's father.

Daniel Andre Green was convicted of first-degree murder, first-degree robbery, and conspiracy in the July 23, 1993, attack on James Jordan, who was killed as he awoke from a nap in his luxury car.

Jordan, 57, had been driving to Charlotte from Wilmington and had parked his $40,000 red Lexus coupe off the highway to take a nap. The car was a gift from his athlete son.

Green had been preparing to rob a motel when the expensive car caught his eye and changed his target. He sneaked up to the car just as Jordan was awakening.

He made a statement like, "What is this?" Or "What's going on?" As soon as these words were out of his mouth, Daniel shot him.

CNN Online

Tex says

We regrouped after Jordan's retirement. Scottie Pippen led the way, and the team won fifty-five ball games. Except for a free throw made on a foul called on Pippen's block in the last seconds of a game with New York, we would have been playing for another championship without Jordan. I thought they did an outstanding job, playing to their full capacity throughout the season. I thought that was Phil's best year in his coaching career. I was proud of everyone.

Tex says

I knew about the closeness between Jordan and his father. I knew how his father motivated and supported his playing. It would be hard, nearly impossible, for Jordan to overcome this. I was not surprised when two days before training camp, Jordan announced his retirement. He needed to get away from the game for a while. He had been playing competitive basketball for years without a break. Despite the fact that he called it retirement, I personally thought he would come back at some point, especially with the successful team play we had developed that took some scoring pressure off him.

United Center, home to the Chicago Bulls, after its opening
August 18, 1994.

The Bulls's next two seasons were filled with trouble. Jordan's
father was murdered. Jordan retired two days before 1993 preseason training was to begin.▲

Problems brewed between players, and two players retired.
The team moved into the Bulls's new arena as well as the new
practice facility, Benton Center, where Tex helped plan and
design the basketball court. Everybody had to cope with welcome
and unwelcome changes.▲

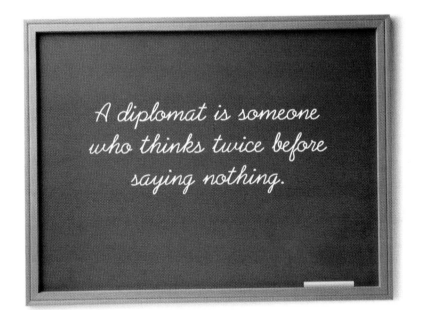

A diplomat is someone who thinks twice before saying nothing.

"I always felt that he was first and foremost sincerely committed to teaching and developing his players, for the season and for their lives. Of course he wanted to win, but that was not his biggest motivation."

Russ Wittberger
Marquette University 1955

Both Jordan and Pippen had reservations about bringing Rodman on initially, but they believed he would be a good asset and a complement to the team. So, at the end, they both wanted him. They said they felt like they could control him, on the floor at least.

Tex says

Jordan returned in March of 1995 and said he would stick with the Triangle for the upcoming season. With Jordan's commitment in place, Tex and Jackson agreed the team could use a powerful rebounding forward. Dennis Rodman had the skills they wanted. He also was unpredictable—neon hair colors, gaudy clothes, random actions—on and off the courts. Tex feared that Rodman could become their biggest problem yet. Jordan and Scottie Pippen, the two players with whom Rodman would play most closely, hesitated. Tex voted No. ▲

Rodman was brought to Chicago for interviews with owners, managers, and coaches. Some connection seemed possible between him and the Bulls organization, especially with Jackson. Rodman accepted an offer for the 1994-95 season.

Chicago fans were shocked. Would Rodman be the power-forward the Bulls needed or a distracting sideshow? Tex remained unsure.

1) Begin drill

4) Next player continues drill

5)

Dennis Rodman joins the Chicago Bulls team. Fans are stunned.

Dennis Rodman , a great
student of rebounding,
developed an uncanny
ability to seize the ball.

cut

Dribble

cut

Pass #2

cut

Pass #1

Tex began to work with Rodman. *This guy has great physical form*, Tex said to himself. *He could have been a world-class quarter-miler or a high hurdler. He can run. He can jump. I can't wear him out.*

Tex noticed that Rodman had trouble concentrating. He lacked mental discipline. Next Tex noticed how self-conscious Rodman was. He even seemed shy at times. When Rodman didn't pay attention and felt uncomfortable with people watching him, Tex knew he would have trouble being a consistent free-throw shooter, especially under pressure.

Tex wanted to improve Rodman's free-throw shooting. As a rebounder, Rodman was sure to draw fouls. The Bulls would need the points.

"In free-throw shooting, you go through the same motions all the time," Tex coached Rodman. "You set yourself on the line, and the shot starts from the floor. For the release of the ball, use the fingers, not the fingertips."

Rodman improved. When he stepped on the basketball court, he was fun to coach, and a challenge, which Tex liked. Off the floor was another story. Tex worried about him all the time.

Tex turned practices into games to get Rodman to concentrate. "OK, the score is tied, and you are fouled, and you have a chance to win the game," Tex would say. "There are three seconds left on the clock, so step up there now, and hit two free throws for me."

Rodman stepped up and shot the free throws, over and over, day after day. Tex didn't give up.

Never as steady as Tex had hoped, Rodman nevertheless became known for his pressure shooting at the foul line. He was a great complement as an outstanding rebounder for the Bulls team. He learned the Triangle quickly. He dedicated himself to it, and the ideas worked for him and the team.

1 *Begin drill*

4 *Next player continues drill*

5

Squaring away the triangle; Winter drilling new Bulls

In its very basic terms, the triangle—or "triple-post" offense—involves all five players sharing the ball and moving. Players have to learn how to react to situations and let their passing and movement find and exploit weak spots in an opposing defense.

"We're sort of in the same situation we were in eight years ago," Winter says. "It was a question of Phil selling Michael and Scottie Pippen, two pretty good basketball players, who Phil felt would have to sacrifice themselves individually in order for us to win championships. Phil was able to do that.

"It took them some time, but Pippen was one of the fastest learners I've every coached and Michael has such a tremendous grasp of the game that it really wasn't that difficult with those players."

The Bulls have six titles to show for it. Winter says it's even more important to have complementary players who understand the offense.

Chicago Tribune, February 1, 1999

If individual skills are not harnessed together properly, the net result is a game of individualism which cannot succeed against a group of coordinated team players of like caliber.

The Bulls finished the 1996 season with 22 wins and 10 losses, the greatest NBA season record of all time. They met the Seattle Supersonics in the finals.

Tex endorsed Jackson's game plan against Seattle—some scoring from Jordan and a lot of ball-sharing among all the players. The Bulls won over the Supersonics in five games. Championship #4.

On a roll, the Bulls faced the Utah Jazz the next year in the 1997 NBA championship finals. Games One and Two came easily enough for the Bulls. The Jazz won Game Three. They won Game Four too, mostly because the Bulls ball boy served up Gator Lode instead of Gatorade. Gator Lode replaces carbohydrates in the body, to be used after a workout. Taken during the game, it caused stomach cramps and forced some of the Bulls off the floor.

The Big Three: Dennis Rodman, left, Michael Jordan, center, and Scottie Pippen, right.

Jordan awoke with a severe flu virus the morning of Game Five. He dragged himself to the Jazz's Delta Center and collapsed after scoring thirty-eight points. Teammates worried. Would he be able to play Game Six? "His discomfort may just create better concentration for him," Tex reassured fans. "He has multiple ways of compensating."

"Dad doesn't give adoration to high-powered athletes, and at the same time he doesn't see anybody as beneath him, or weird, or wasting his time. I remember a game I was playing in during the LA NBA Pro Summer League. He told everyone after the last game, "You are all great basketball players, and you all have great careers ahead of you. Your future may be in the NBA, or it may be City or YMCA leagues or it may be street-ball. It doesn't matter to me, and it shouldn't matter to you. It's basketball any way you look at it, and it's been a privilege to coach you the way I think it should be played."

Chris Winter

Chris Winter
Fred "Tex's" Middle Son

Scottie Pippen shines in the title win over the Utah Jazz.

Tex says Scottie Pippen's back spasms nearly kept him out of Game Six with the Utah Jazz in the playoffs 1998. Jordan agreed to play the entire forty-eight minutes without Pippen. Jordan scored forty-five points, and Pippen played just enough to assist Jordan's game-winning shot to push the score, 87-86. It was the Bulls's sixth championship in eight seasons. A tremendous record. It was also Jordan's last shot for the Bulls. He retired from the Bulls the next January, giving tribute to me for the development of his mental skills that helped drive him on his quest for excellence.

Michael Jordan and Tex share a moment of mutual respect.

With Game Six tied and only seconds left, Jordan saw teammate Steve Kerr in position to shoot. Tex sprang to his feet. What would Jordan do? Shoot his famous jump shot? Fire a chest pass to Kerr? Tex watched the Jazz players close in on Jordan, ready to block his final shot in any way they could. Fans and players whooped and hollered. So did Tex.

Jordan passed to Kerr. Swish. Team play, a reminder of the previous playoffs with the Phoenix Suns when the ball went from Jordan to Grant to Paxson, who sank a three-point shot to win the championship. Now Kerr had nailed the Bulls's fifth championship. Tex's innovation, the Triangle, performed by Jordan and company, looked like art on a canvas and ballet on a stage. Spectacular.

Tex slapped Jordan a victory high-five and grinned as if he knew what the next year would bring. Jordan and the Bulls, using the Triangle, would beat the Utah Jazz again in 1998 for their sixth NBA championship. Who would have guessed that Jordan's game-winning jump shot to win that sixth title, with a Scottie Pippen assist—who spent most of the game on a training table suffering back spasms—would be Jordan's final shot of his incredible career. Sweet satisfaction. The power of team. Sweaty hugs all around. ▲

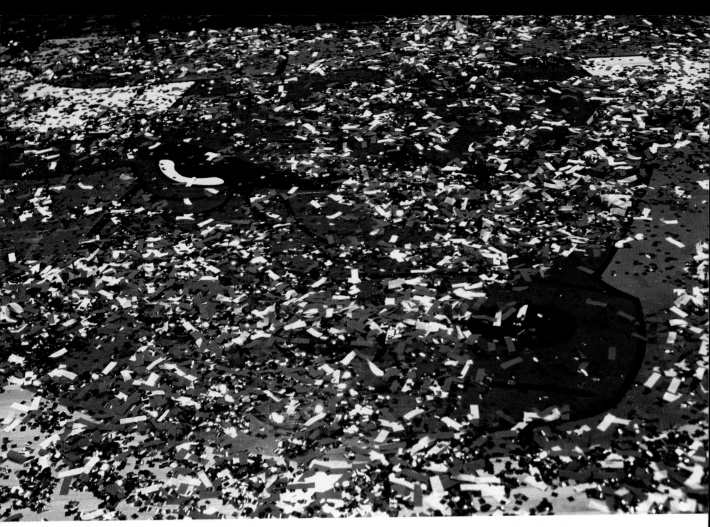

The United Center exploded into celebration following the title victory over the Utah Jazz.

"Notwithstanding Tex's career in a high pressure, stressful profession, he always maintained consistency with his emotions. His great focus on fundamentals and strategy, instead of a 'winning at all costs' approach, kept him mentally and physically strong."

Joe Vader
Kansas State University 1961

Offensive Build-Up Drills

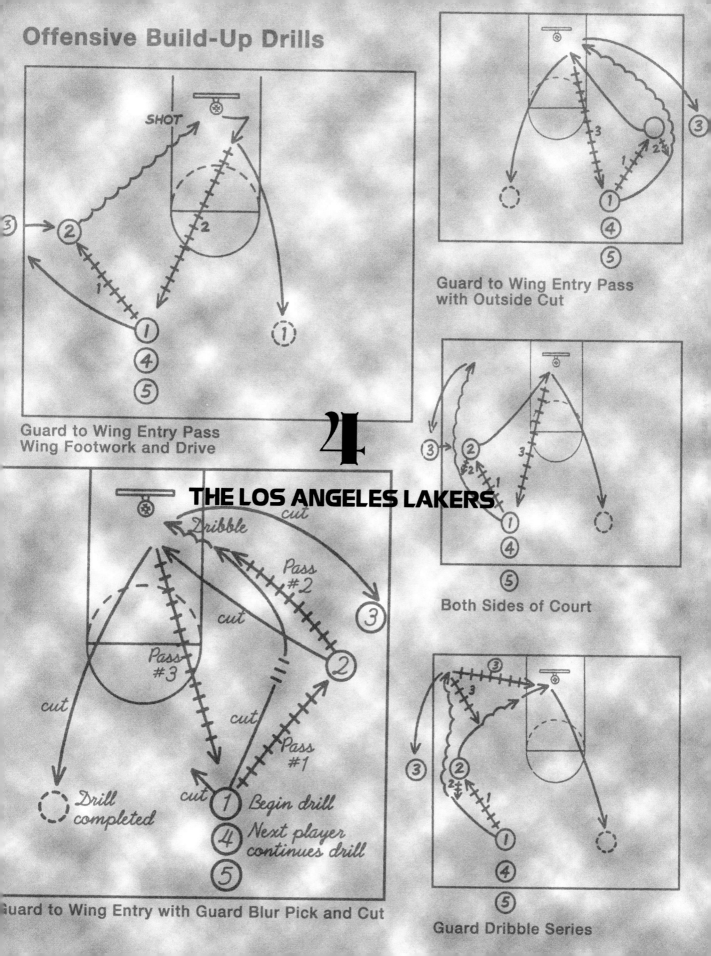

Guard to Wing Entry Pass with Outside Cut

Guard to Wing Entry Pass Wing Footwork and Drive

4

THE LOS ANGELES LAKERS

SHOT

Both Sides of Court

Dribble

cut

Pass #2

cut

Pass #3

cut

Pass #1

cut

Drill completed

cut

Begin drill

Next player continues drill

Guard to Wing Entry with Guard Blur Pick and Cut

Guard Dribble Series

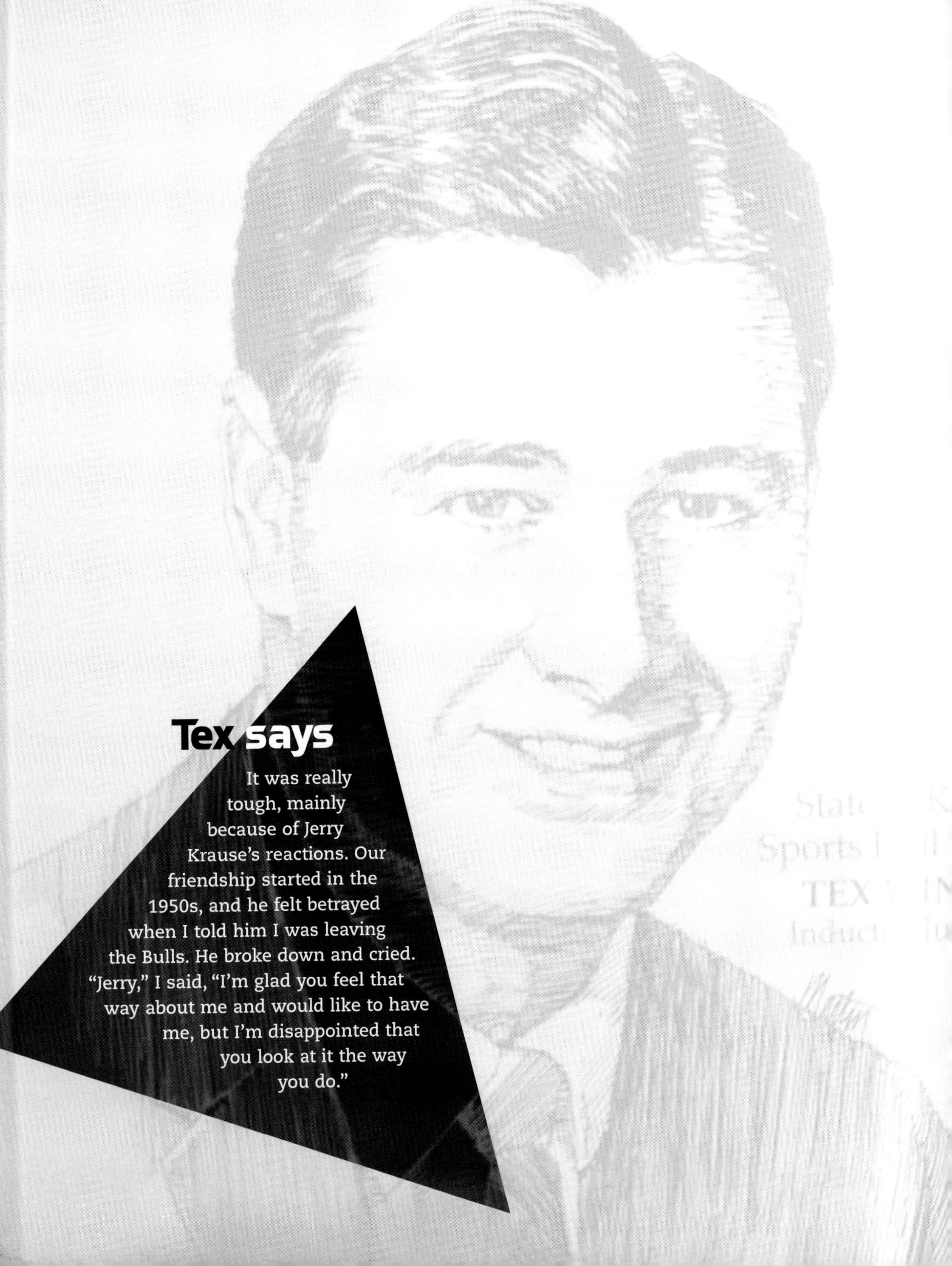

Tex says

It was really
tough, mainly
because of Jerry
Krause's reactions. Our
friendship started in the
1950s, and he felt betrayed
when I told him I was leaving
the Bulls. He broke down and cried.
"Jerry," I said, "I'm glad you feel that
way about me and would like to have
me, but I'm disappointed that
you look at it the way
you do."

"I still look forward to coming to work," he says simply when asked why, at 77, he's still coaching. "Practices, particularly, I like."

But Winter has a little secret. He loves this: The explaining, the demonstrating, the yelling, the wondering if they're ever going to get it right.

"That's my job. To teach and to coach," said Winter, who will receive the National Association of Basketball Coaches' Golden Anniversary Award this weekend.

The Topeka Capital-Journal Sunday, March 28, 1999

Tex Winter, assistant coach for offense, Los Angeles Lakers.

Nancy Winter, Tex's wife.

Tex stayed with the Bulls one more season as assistant to the new head coach, Tim Floyd. Jackson had left at the end of the 1998 season. It wasn't the same, even though Tex worked well with Floyd. Tex and Jackson had a rhythm, and now it was gone.

Following the season with the Bulls, Tex and Nancy traveled to Greece. Sight-seeing, basketball clinics, and talk about the future filled their time. After taking one year off, Jackson had asked Tex to join him with the Los Angeles Lakers where Jackson had become head coach.

Stay with the Bulls? Go to Los Angeles?

"I feel very flattered to have two great franchises interested in my services," Tex told reporters when they returned from Greece, "but at my age, I probably should be looking at the nursing home next door." Tex was seventy-seven years old.

A few days later, Tex left a note for Nancy on the kitchen table saying he had gone to the office to tell Floyd and Jerry Krause that he was leaving the Bulls. "I wasn't surprised," Nancy told friends, "although I knew this was the hardest basketball decision he had ever made."▲

Tex's time-tested triangle

As an NBA assistant, Winter brought the triangle to the Chicago Bulls, and the organization had the most successful run of any pro team since the 1960 Celtics, winning six championships in eight years.

When the Lakers lured former Bulls coach Phil Jackson out of retirement, he persuaded Winter to move West, which brought the triangle full circle in a way. Winter's coaching influences are from southern California, where he went to high school and first studied the game. The result of the export? Los Angeles won a team-record 67 games in a regular season.

The basic setup of Winter's triangle is three players taking positions near the sideline, foul line, and basket on the same side of the floor. The scheme's philosophy is just as important. It's more read-and-react than attack, though you didn't get that impression watching O'Neal drop 43 points on the Pacers.

"Taking what the defense makes available is part of the triangle," Winter said, "O'Neal put himself in positions to score."

By Blair Kerkhoff,
The Kansas City Star, June 20, 2000

Tex says

I credit our success to Phil's ability to handle stress. When things went wrong, he would leave players in the game to solve the problem on their own. I would say, "Coach, get a time out, man. Don't just sit there. Get up and start earning that fabulous salary!" And then I would watch him smile at my badgering while the players figured out what to do. I've told him I was not only his consultant. I was also his "insultant." For some reason, I got by with talking to him that way—which I did in private, not in front of the team.

There are not many head coaches, especially after establishing the credibility Phil has, who would put up with me. It takes a special guy. I'm very fortunate. Except for Phil, I would have been long gone from NBA basketball.

A desire to win, to play as a team, submerging the self for the benefit of the group to attain perfection, and to put their powers to the utmost will turn a merely mediocre team into a team of poise, judgment, and determination.

After winning a third championship with the Lakers in 2002, the organization made rings for players and the coaching staff in honor of Tex. The jewel-encrusted piece has several triangle designs on the front.

"The reason I love Tex so much is that he's just so open and all he sees is basketball. I mean that's all he cares about. The first thing he said when he got here was, 'I don't criticize the individual. I criticize the act.' He's constantly on me about the game. He's on everybody about the game, but that's what he cares about, and that's what I love about him."

Kobe Bryant
Los Angeles Lakers

In their first season with the Lakers, the coaching staff pulled the team together. With Shaquille O'Neal and Kobe Bryant leading the way, the Lakers grabbed first place in the league and won the 2000 NBA championship over the Indiana Pacers in six games. This was the seventh championship for Tex and Jackson as coaching partners. Tex was excited.

Using the Triangle offense, the Lakers won Championship #8 against the Philadelphia 76ers in 2001.

Charged up by the successes of the two previous seasons, the Lakers beat the New Jersey Nets for their third consecutive championship. "Two Three-Peats with the Bulls and now a Three-Peat with the Lakers," Tex told Jackson. "We could start a jewelry business with all the diamonds and rubies in our nine championship rings." ▲

Coach Winter with superstars
Kobe Bryant, left, and
Shaquille O'Neal, right.

cut
Dribble
Pass
#2
3
2
cut
Pass
#1
Begin drill
drill

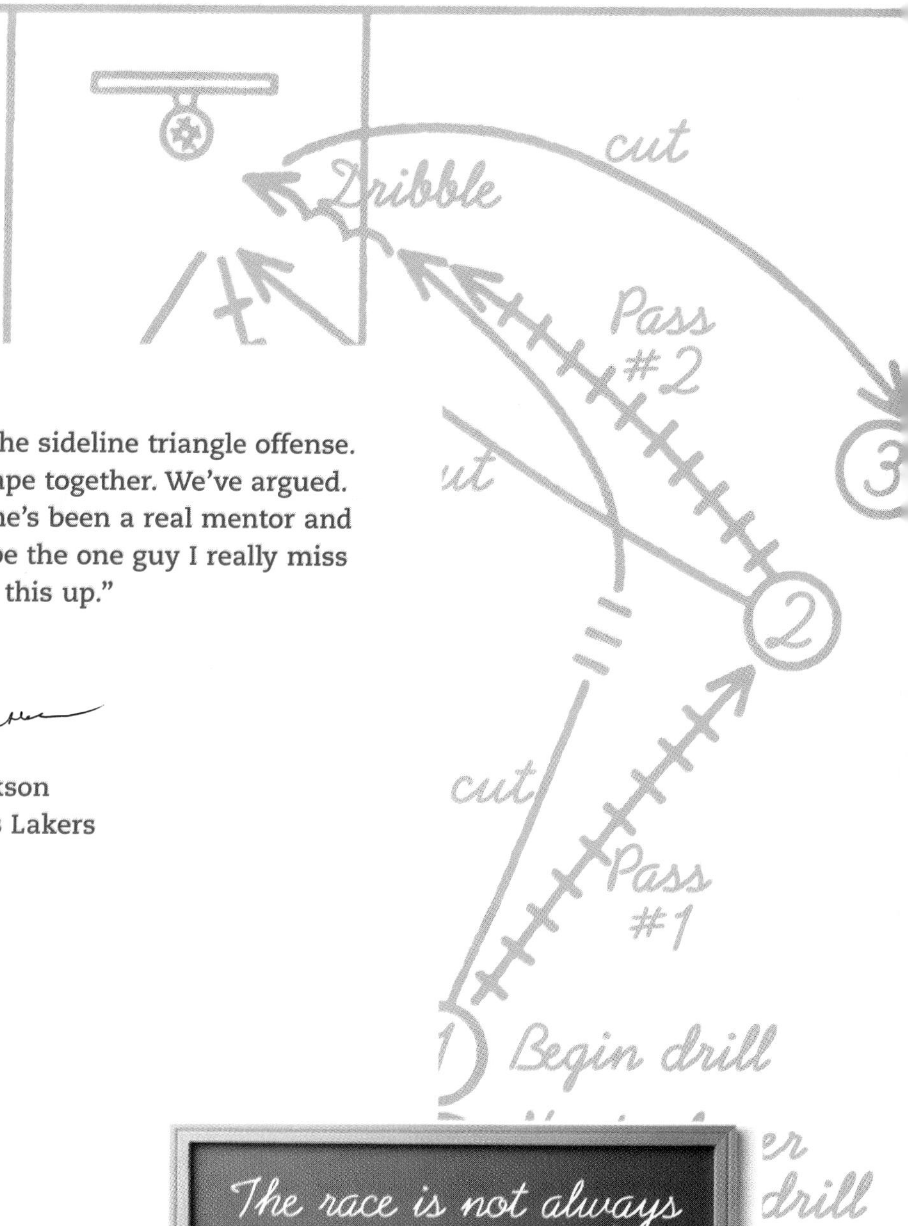

"Tex Winter's the innovator of the sideline triangle offense. We've watched a lot of game tape together. We've argued. We've cajoled each other, and he's been a real mentor and compatriot to me. He's gonna be the one guy I really miss when I hang this up."

Phil Jackson
Los Angeles Lakers

Foot surgery slowed O'Neal during the first half of the 2002-03 season. The team kept winning as Bryant scored at least thirty points in sixteen straight games and at least forty points in nine consecutive games. They met the San Antonio Spurs for the championship playoffs. In Game Six, the Spurs pulled away in the fourth quarter to stop the Lakers's three-year championship run. The Spurs won, 110-82.

The race is not always
to the swift, nor the
battle to the strong,
but that's not a bad
way to bet.

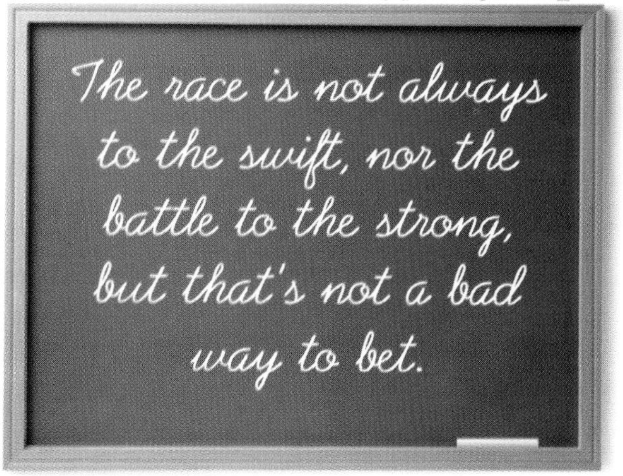

Coach Winter during an
interview, explaining his
Triangle offense.

"In all of the years at Kansas State he had
only a couple of pro players but won
championships eight times."

Roger Craft
Roger Craft
Kansas State University

Tex says

From a
coaching
standpoint,
sometimes more can
be accomplished from
losses than from wins. It's
human nature to love to win.
Players get high and don't want to talk
about corrections. Oftentimes, it's
harder to get a team's attention
when they win than when
they lose. I've found that
to be an interesting
phenomenon about
coaching.

"Tex has a very good mind. He looked at our competition and decided what to do. UCLA was a big, tall team and tried to trap their competition by passing over their heads. We were effective against them because Tex said we were not going to pass. We were going to dribble the ball. He also got us in shape for basketball by playing basketball, not running laps. That way we knew what it felt like to shoot the basketball with tired legs from playing basketball, not running laps. Under Tex, the average player became good. The good player became better. The very good player became really great."

Rafael Stone
University of Washington 1970

What went wrong when the Lakers were within inches of another title, Tex asked himself. "I can't say that I was confident about the players' desire to improve," Tex told colleagues. "I went back to the first principle for learning the Triangle—The Law of Readiness: the more ready you are to learn the game, the better you will do and the faster you will pick it up."▲

Tex had been puzzled about O'Neal's performance from the beginning. "He's a really good person for the Lakers in a lot of ways," Tex said, "but I don't understand him. And I don't think he understands me either."

"I'm doing OK," O'Neal would say when Tex tried to inspire him. "Look at the money I'm making."

Tex had seen it happen many times. "The superstars build huge egos," Tex told reporters. "People praise them. People cater to them, telling them how great they are. Pretty soon, the stars start believing that about themselves. Then the money becomes their proof. Coaching, correcting, and teaching become difficult."

Game 5: Lakers 87–Pistons 100

The dream is over for the Lakers and it could mean the end of the Jackson-Shaq-Kobe era. Detroit was clearly the best team of the Finals and won the NBA Championship with a 100-87 victory. Chauncey Billups was the Finals MVP with 21 points and 5.2 assists per game. The Lakers proved they're human and showed the worst version of this team. Kobe took too many shots and missed most of them. Shaq missed 10 of 16 free throws. The other Lakers didn't contribute and Jackson couldn't find an answer to the problem. Now an agitated summer with big questions is ahead: Will Bryant, Jackson, Malone, and Payton be part of the team next year?

Lakers Web, June 15, 2004

"Tex Winter is a pioneer of the game of basketball. He's been involved in so many innovations of the game: strategy, teaching the game, formatting offense. He's the most dedicated to the game of anyone I've every known or known about. With his appetite for learning this game, he's still—sixty years later —always looking for something new."

Jim Wooldridge, Head Basketball Coach
Kansas State University 2006

Tex says

A big factor was Malone's age and his injuries both early and later in the season. He never really recovered. He was a great rebounder. It was a sad time for him. I felt so sorry for him.

He was also a great leader. I remember when Karl came to a practice and found Shaq on an exercise bicycle. "Get busy," he told Shaq. "I didn't come down here to watch you ride a bike."

Shaq needed someone like that, which is different from a coach telling him the same thing, especially me.

As the 2003-04 season began, the Lakers added Hall of Famers Karl Malone and Gary Payton. "I think this is a mistake," Tex said when asked his opinion. "Their playing habits are entrenched. They're great players, but they are not the players they were a couple of years ago. They're on the downhill side of their careers."

But the public's interpretation was different. They thought the Lakers had put together one of the most talented and experienced teams in NBA history. What couldn't they do now? Expectations were too high, Tex thought. Some said that if this team didn't win the championship, there ought to be an investigation.▲

Tex and Jackson were ready to work the Triangle offense that had been so successful in the past. Then, two major problems messed up things: Bryant's distraction with a sexual assault charge and an ugly competition that developed between Bryant and O'Neal. The problems pulled the team apart. The Lakers lost to the Detroit Pistons in the championship finals.

Lakers coaching staff:
Left to right:
Kurt Rambis,
Jim Cleamons,
Phil Jackson,
Frank Hamblen,
Tex Winter.

The team with the most possibilities fell apart. Tex often said there is no substitute for hustle. Exceptional talent did not make up for bad relationships, injuries, lack of focus, and neglected work. The magic was over.

Wildcats' Winter up for Hall of Fame

Every year, Phil Jackson gets a letter from the Hall of Fame, asking him for a nice donation. Every year, he sends back the same response: Induct Tex Winter, then maybe we'll talk.

The folks in Springfield, Mass. have considered Winter's candidacy six times. Somehow, his credentials have been deemed insufficient time and again. Winter, a Los Angeles Lakers assistant coach, is again a finalist; the Hall will announce this year's inductees today.

Winter's induction would mean a lot to Jackson, who considers him a mentor and a close friend. And, he notes, "It would mean I might give a contribution to the Hall of Fame. Other than that, they're failing in their job to hold up what the Hall of Fame really means," Jackson said.

The Chicago Bulls won six championships using Winter's famed triangle offense, and the Lakers have won the past three using it. Winter has coached 56 consecutive seasons at the collegiate and pro levels, an achievement in itself.

The Hall's voting process is shrouded in secrecy. The selection committee members are all unidentified and not even known to one another. Bulls general manager Jerry Krause quit his Hall membership in part because of the process and Winter's exclusion.

"Tex was a legitimate, outstanding coach in every right," Jackson said.

By Howard Beck, Los Angeles Daily News, April 7, 2003

A team is not in danger if it has possession of the ball and knows what to do with it.

Tex says

With the big egos we had on that Lakers team, and their being used to having their own way— run and gun, taking all the shots they wanted—they gave the Triangle half effort. And it didn't work. There were a couple of times when the players got desperate, and they gave the Triangle approach more attention. The results spoke for themselves. In spite of all this, injuries played a key role, especially for Karl Malone. Had he not been hurt, we still had a chance. I can only imagine what those players—Shaq and Kobe and others—could have accomplished with team play. But things splintered away from what we really wanted, even with the same players who had made it happen the year before. I saw it. I felt it. When a team wins championships, the egos get bigger. They say success breeds success. But to me, success also breeds complacency, a cockiness instead of confidence. That hurt us.

Coach Winter, far left, taking notes for the Lakers next practice session. Assistant coaches Kurt Rambis, Frank Hamblen, and Gary Vitti, trainer, fill the bench.

For Tex, that last season, 2003-04 with the Lakers, was one of his toughest. He hated to see all that talent wasted on false egos and personal problems. He believed in taking care of things, and that included player talents.

Tex still loved the game, and he still loved to work with those who respected themselves and their abilities. "That's what we are meant to do," he said, "develop our best talents and use them for the good of the whole team."

Tex announced his retirement after the All-Star break in February. "I told Phil and our general manager that this was my last year, that I planned to retire when the season ended so they could plan accordingly."

Jackson announced his retirement at the end of the season.

I handled stress in a strange way when I'd get nervous before each pole vault. I would take a pallet or mat to the track and take a nap during the thirty to forty-five minutes between vaults. My teammates knew I did this. They'd wake me for the next jump. I apply that habit all around. In basketball during stressful times, I shrug my shoulders, let my whole body slump, and relax. After a big game, because I can do this, I go home and go to sleep. When asked my secret to longevity, I tell people I've hibernated away half my life. I do believe sleep, rest, and relaxation are important, especially for athletes and coaches.

Tex says

"I'm in the advertising business, and one day we were sitting around trying to figure out how to explain something complex for IBM. We came up with the idea of using basketball as a metaphor and I immediately thought of Tex and the Triangle offense. The client loved the idea. We called Tex. He came down, and we shot the spot at a gym in an insane asylum, if you can believe that, and Tex was just great—just himself. It was an odd moment—twenty-five years after I'd played for him, sitting in this gym, and he didn't look like he'd aged a day. The commercial came out great and ran a lot."

Chris Wall
Northwestern 1978

> "Tex's greatest strength is his ability to analyze during a game and make necessary adjustments to win."

Ernie D. Barrett

Ernie Barrett
Kansas State University 1951

From the days of regrouping after his father's death in 1932 to discovering the joy of success for the team's sake at a junior high track meet, Tex grew more convinced that there was more to be taught and learned than how to win. From the first time he saw Loyola of Los Angeles basketball players depend on each other during practices at Huntington Park High School, he began collecting ideas that later became his Triangle offense. Help people find out what they do best, he advocated, and build on those skills. Put the players together with a plan. Watch them create plays, outwit the defense, and score because of their combined efforts. Share the work and share the glory. Get over the idea that one person contributes more than another.

Tex worked very hard. Some of the team situations he took on seemed doomed from the start. Others allowed him to move right in to teach the Triangle. Neither response dampened his beliefs.▲ Each time he encountered a new combination of players, he

A bust of Coach Winter made by a former player, Hayden Abbott.

Bill Guthridge, Tex Winter, and Roy DeWitz.

Many of my college players went into coaching. I'm proud of that. I encouraged Bill Guthridge, a Kansas State player and my assistant coach, to join Dean Smith at the University of North Carolina. He did a great job for me, but those were some of our poorer years. He was highly organized and worked very hard at recruiting. He was key in recruiting Michael Jordan to North Carolina. Guthridge led the North Carolina team to learn the Triangle system of team ball and became head coach after Smith's retirement.

Norm Stewart at the University of Missouri wanted Roy DeWitz, another Kansas State player, to teach his team the Triangle concepts. In both cases, I insisted they go.

"When I was Tex's assistant coach, my scouting report noted a Tulsa University player who 'went right.' We were beaten by this player's 'going left' and I was grilled at a Wildcat Club meeting about the report. Tex stood up and stated that he supported the scouting report and that any good player should know that an opposing good player will take the opportunities you give him. To me, that was an example of Tex telling the truth and standing behind his assistant."

Roy DeWitz
Kansas State University 1958

142

Coach Winter, chosen Coach of the Century by Kansas State basketball fans, joined by members of the Team of the Century on March 1, 2003. Back row: Bob Boozer; Jack Parr; Chuckie Williams; Mike Evans; Rolando Blackman; Ed Nealy; Mike Henson, Steve Henson's father. Front row: Ernie Barrett; Pat Hartman, Jack Hartman's wife; Tex Winter; Lon Kruger; Jim Gardner, Jack Gardner's son.

found the Triangle was flexible enough to wrap itself around the team's unique makeup if the players were committed. If they weren't, Tex reminded himself that some wanted basketball to be a personal sport.

"I had high spots and low spots along the way with players and teams," Tex said, "but the most gratifying situation was my college teaching and coaching when I saw young men develop from their freshman years through their senior years. I'd have to say the Kansas State teams of 1957-58 and 1958-59 executed the Triangle better than any other—even the pros. They depended on each other. They were unselfish in their play."

"It is just amazing that what Tex taught college players in the fifties and sixties is working even better today. He was a man truly ahead of his time and is still coming up with new variations of the Triangle offense for modern day basketball."

George Schultz, Jr.

George Schultz, Jr.
Kansas State University 1969

Jimmy Needles, developer of the first triangle alignment Tex observed, called "Reverse Action."

Sam Barry, Tex's coach at USC who also used triangle alignment, which he called "Center Opposite."

I liked how Phil described the essence of the Triangle. He said it was a way to play into the opponent's energy. If the defense applies pressure in one spot, Phil and I told our players to step into the opening on the other side. "This is different than running preplanned plays," Phil told our players. We wanted to see every player creating a play on the floor, moment after moment, by watching and taking cues from the defense. "Read the defense," we said.

Tex says Sam Barry and Jimmy Needles were the beginning of it all for me—the sideline triangle (overload) alignment. They were great coaches. Needles became basketball coach for the 1936 Olympics in Berlin, the first time basketball was featured in the Olympics where they played on outdoor, sometimes muddy courts. And of course, Barry became a very successful coach at USC. The Triangle offense has evolved over the years, so of course, neither coach would recognize some of what we do now.

The Offense Even Bulls Don't Understand

"None of this would be where it is if it wasn't for Phil," Winter said in a gentle Texas twang. "People talk about Tex Winter's offense. That's not so. It's my thinking, and that's what I'm paid for. But Phil's the guy who has to implement it. If he didn't want to do it, we wouldn't be doing it. He's accepted the philosophy.

"My ambition is to leave a legacy of my philosophy of basketball with someone. And I appreciate very, very much the opportunity Phil has given me to do that. He has accepted a great deal of it, and what he accepts is his from now on. Just as what I accepted from my coaches is mine. Phil has added things, and he has taken things away. That is how the game grows."

By Dave Hoekstra, Chicago Sun Times, Sunday, December 23, 1990

Coach Winter outlines Lakers's strategy for Assistant Coach Frank Hamblen and Head Coach Jackson.

Jackson's dedication to the Triangle kept Tex's thinking fresh. "I would re-examine why I believed in the system and how I could teach players to make it work even better with the team we had," Tex said. "I felt like an innovator, one of my favorite roles."▲

Coach Winter, running Basketball 101, an annual event sponsored by the Lakers for corporate sponsors and season ticket holders who want to learn more about the Triangle offense.

"If we are the sum of the contributions of all who have crossed our paths, Tex's contribution to my life is incalculable."

Jack Parr
Kansas State University 1958

Tex says

Many new coaches wouldn't want me. They coach only one way. That's what they have to do. Many would say, "The Triangle offense—it's good, yeah, it's real good—but I don't know it, so I'm not going to try it." They're right. It takes a lot of time. You must thoroughly understand it before you can teach it.

Sometimes it's hard for me to believe that some coaches do make a commitment to study the Triangle offense. I admire anyone who takes on a new way, especially if they've had success in an old way. It's the slight edge. When coaches use the Triangle, they know what went right or wrong and why. No guesswork. Rudyard Kipling said it best, "I keep six honest serving-men (They taught me all I knew); Their names are What and Why and When and How and Where and Who."

146

Coach Winter poses in front of his Kansas State Hall of Fame picture where he began his basketball coaching career.

Tex spent nearly sixty seasons as a coach developing and teaching the Triangle. 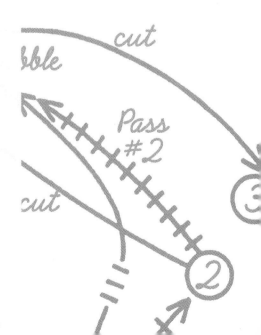 "Winning is what sports is about, especially in pro sports," he told an interviewer. "But far more important is how teammates count on each other to do that winning. Basketball is a team game, I've always said. I'd like to leave that legacy."

Dear Readers,

Here are a few more comments about Tex:

DIGGER

No matter what Tex does, he works hard. His son Brian remembers. "There was seldom a time he did something at home without coming away with cuts, scrapes, bruises or blisters. When he was exhausted, he would drop, and after a short rest, he would be back up again in constant motion."

His son Chris agrees, "Dad's very educated about athletic ability. Dad recognized that he was good at sports and found a way to work hard in a fun environment."

BLIND

Tex does not see color, size, affluence, or stardom. "Dad is unpretentious," Russ, his oldest son, says. "He believes in people's goodness. After Dad had coached a Kansas State game, I saw him go over to a mentally-challenged kid who was being pushed aside, calmly talk to him, and stay with him while he settled down. Dad is genuine and gracious with everyone."

LASER MIND

Tex does not waste time or resources. When he sees others not taking good care of their minds and bodies, he feels pain. To him, life is about being focused—laser-minded—doing your best. He thinks like a master engineer; he solves problems and moves forward.

Tex:

- makes full use of what he has, such as three players and a triangle to stymie the competition.
- avoids taking credit because he believes team effort outdoes one person's efforts.
- ignores barriers between himself and others because he doesn't see them.
- is passionate about teaching for best performance. Sloppy playing doesn't cut it with him.

Tex's dedication to hard work and excellence reveal who he is and what he has accomplished. My hope is that you have been inspired in some way, large or small, by the stories and events you've just read. You and I, as participants in this book, are witnesses to Tex's legacy as teacher and coach, a legacy which will live on through all who have known him.

Ann Parr

Ann Parr

Tex's former players talk about their coach's attributes:

GENEROSITY

"Coach Winter called me into his office and told me that my chances of playing that year were limited. He said the choice to remain on the team was mine. He also felt that he owed me an education. I would receive a books and tuition scholarship regardless of my decision. He didn't have to do that, but he did."

John Olson, Kansas State University

"When a clinic was completed at Bethany College, Tex spent time talking to our players and signing autographs. Rod, a guard from Texas, asked Tex where he could get some NBA socks like Tex had on. Tex said, 'You can have these if you want to wash them.' He sits down, takes off his shoes and socks, and gives his socks to Rod. Rod told Tex he would never wash them, just put them on his wall."

Clair Oleen, Bethany College-Lindsborg, Kansas

"Tex is just Tex and has always known me, my late Dad, and 91-year-old mom by our first names. He always seems genuinely happy to see us."

Bob Boyd, Kansas State University

"Tex contributed to my success in two ways. First, by allowing me to try out for the team, he showed me that you should allow anyone with a reasonable chance of success to compete for the opportunity to succeed. Second, by his honesty in dealing with me, he taught me that you should always tell people where they stand and help them re-channel their efforts."

Bill Sinderson, Kansas State University

PRIORITIES

"Tex said that if you can't pass you can't play. He meant passing in the classroom and passing the ball."

Al Peithman, Kansas State University

"He was particular about every detail. For example, he taught coming to a stop from dribbling with both feet so that either foot could be the pivot foot to make various moves."

Erick Siverling, Marquette University

"Near the end of the season I got into a fight with a teammate, and Tex sent me to the shower. I was not to return until I had 'my act together.' This was Tuesday, and we had a road game Saturday. Tex let me on the bus with nothing said, and I played one of my best games ever. Tex understood that young people will make wrong-headed decisions and need second chances."

Gene Stauffer, Kansas State University

"One day in practice, Tex called all the players over to the bleachers. He said, 'The difference between the best players out here today and the rest of you is very little. Any one of you could start Friday night if you show me in practice this week that you want to play'."

John Englemann, Kansas State University

"Coach Winter had a scholarship player who was rated as one of the top players in the nation, and when this player was disruptive, he had to forfeit his scholarship. Tex would not stand for any undisciplined player who was not willing to sacrifice for the team."

Bob George, Kansas State University

"Tex taught us to be thrifty. Other teams had steak for pre-game meals. We had melba toast and tea."

Dale Sevcik, Marquette University

CHARACTER

"Coach Winter convinced my mother that he was the kind of man her son should play for."

Dick Knostman, Kansas State University

"Players who didn't have the commitment and focus were gone—regardless of what anyone else thought."

Lou Poma, Kansas State University

"Tex came to our house. My dad thought he was the paper boy, collecting. Tex stayed for an hour. My dad lit his pipe, with me wanting to know what he thought. He finally said he thought the other schools were fine, but Mr. Winter was a real gentleman. 'I'd be proud to have you play ball for him.' The next week I became the first player Tex recruited as a head basketball coach."   *Russ Wittberger, Marquette University*

"Tex made me realize the importance of being a team player to be successful. It goes without saying that everyone who played for Tex was the star of their high school team and needed a team adjustment to play for the Wildcats."

Larry Cohan, Kansas State University

FUN

"Coach Winter loves the game, and it's obvious that he knows the game as well as anyone. I smile when I think of the unique basketball terms he coined, such as 'down the gut,' 'blind pig,' and 'forward pinch'."

David Lawrence, Kansas State University

"Dad's life is about work. Since it might not be fun to work, he's found something fun and works at it. For example, when I was on the Northwestern team with him, he would put up a net and have the team play volleyball. It broke the tediousness of practice, and we'd go play a good game against some competitor."

Chris Winter, Tex's son

TEACHER

"He was a teacher of basketball who used practices as the classroom and games as exams. He did this without ever berating or demeaning his players. He was also a student of the game and was always open to new ideas from assistants and players."   *Richard Schwab, Marquette Universtiy*

"In an Iowa State game we ran a play that defeated them, so the next year, went to the second option, which completely fooled them and resulted in an easy score. Tex taught us that there is no security in this game. And that the same rule applies to whatever we do in life."   *Mike Wroblewski, Kansas State University*

"Tex recognized the few talents that I had and was able to let me use and improve them. He became a father role model for me as my father had died when I was in high school."

Pat McKenzie, Kansas State University

"In 1952, Tex decided to take nine freshmen and one senior to the National Catholic Invitational Tournament in New York. Since we did not have a good year, he was building for the future. His move did not sit well with all the other seniors, juniors, and sophomores. However, we won three games and the title. It was Marquette's first national championship. Tex has been successful wherever he has coached."   *Robert Walczak, Marquette University*

"Ahearn was new. I asked Tex how it was. 'Great place to play, but not for practice. We lost our wall to practice catching.' Next week I brought him the first TossBack. It all started from his simple comment."

Ken Mahoney, Kansas State University

"Tex had an uncanny ability to read offense and defense. He could, in thirty to forty minutes of practice, take us reserves (players number eleven to fifteen) and teach us the next opponent's offense and defense."

Perk Reitemeier, Kansas State University

"To this day, Tex has notes on every player he has ever coached."   *Bob Rousey, Kansas State University*

JUSTICE

"I believe Tex had a difficult time with some alumni and college supporters when he began playing more than two African American athletes at the same time. The 60s brought significant change to college athletics and Tex made the leap."   *Sam Robinson, Kansas State University*

"We walked into a hotel in Houston, and the next thing we knew, we were on our way to the outskirts of town to another motel. I didn't learn until later that Tex was told that one of our teammates would not be served because he was black. So we ALL went to where he would be served. No great fuss was made. 'It just doesn't work that way,' Tex said."

Dean Plagge, Kansas State University

CHRONOLOGY
Fred "Tex" Winter

February 25, 1922	Birth of twins, Morice Fredrick and Mona Francis Winter in Wellington, Texas.
Summer 1929	The Winter family moves to Lubbock, Texas.
December 18, 1932	Death of Marion Ernest Winter, Tex's father.
Summer 1936	Winter family moves to Huntington Park, California.
Mid-term 1940	Tex graduates from Huntington Park High School.
Fall 1940	Tex attends Compton Junior College.
Fall 1942	Tex attends Oregon State University where he plays basketball and pole vaults.
Spring 1943	Tex joins the Navy Aviation V-5 program.
December 1945	Tex discharged from the Navy and returns to Compton Junior College.
Spring 1946	Tex admitted to USC, transferring credits earned from the Navy V-5 program, on both basketball and track scholarships along with the GI Bill.
July 11, 1946	Tex and Nancy Bohnenkamp marry in LaGrande, Oregon.
June 1947	Tex graduates from USC.

Summer 1947	Tex takes job as Gardner's assistant on July 4 and jokes that the fireworks in Manhattan, Kansas celebrate his decision.
January 6, 1950	First son, Russell, is born.
Spring 1951	Kansas State wins the Big Seven. Beat in the NCAA finals by Kentucky.
Fall 1951	Tex replaces Bill Chandler, head basketball coach since 1931 at Marquette University in Milwaukee, Wisconsin.
May 18, 1953	Second son, Christopher, is born.
Fall 1953	Tex returns to Kansas State University to replace Gardner who goes to the University of Utah. Tex builds the best regular season record of any coach in conference history.
February 26, 1955	Third son, Brian, is born.
Fall 1956	Kansas State University beats University of Kansas to win Conference at Dr. Phog Allen's last game at Allen Fieldhouse, University of Kansas.
Spring 1958	Kansas State wins the Big Seven, NCAA Midwest Regionals, earns Kansas State's first national ranking as #1 throughout the season, finishes season as #3, and advances to the NCAA Final Four; falls to Seattle.
	Tex named Coach of the Year by United Press International.
Spring 1959	Kansas State team ranked #1 nationally by both major polls, UPI and AP, the first time in history that both polls choose the same team.

Spring 1962	Tex finishes his book, *Triple Post Offense,* published by Prentice-Hall.
Spring 1964	Tex's 200th win in 11 seasons.
September 29, 1964	Tex's brother Ernest is killed in traffic accident in Lawton, Oklahoma.
Spring 1968	Tex coaches Olympic basketball trials in Colorado Springs. Tex is named NCAA Coach of the Year. Tex leaves Kansas State with 262 wins 117 losses, one of the best records in college coaching. As assistant and head coach, he won eight conference titles, qualified for the NCAA tournament six times, won the Midwest Regional Championship twice, and produced four All-Americans. Tex moves to University of Washington as head basketball coach.
Spring 1971	Tex recruited by Pete Newell to replace Alex Hannum as head coach of the NBA San Diego Rockets team. The team immediately moves to Houston. Key players were Elvin Hayes and Rudy Tomjanovich.
Fall 1973	Tex becomes head basketball coach at Northwestern University in Chicago, Illinois.
Fall 1978	Tex becomes head basketball coach at Long Beach State.
Spring 1983	Tex serves as president of the National Association of Basketball Coaches. Uses his position to upgrade NCAA functioning.
Fall 1983	Tex becomes basketball assistant/consultant under Dale Brown at Louisiana State University. Tex prepares to retire.

Fall 1985	Jerry Krause, general manager for the NBA Chicago Bulls team, hires Tex as assistant coach for offense.
Fall 1987	Krause hires Phil Jackson as assistant coach.
Fall 1989	Phil Jackson becomes head coach for the Bulls. Tex delays retirement at age 67. Bulls win six national championships between 1991 and 1998.
Fall 1991	Tex inducted into the Kansas State University Sports Hall of Fame.
Spring 1997	Tex inducted into the Kansas Sports Hall of Fame.
Fall 2000	Phil Jackson becomes head coach for the NBA Los Angeles Lakers team.
	Tex joins Phil Jackson as assistant coach for offense, is named the 23rd recipient of the John Bunn Award, and granted the Hillyard Anniversary Award for 50 years of outstanding service to the game of basketball by the National Association of Basketball Coaches.
Winter 2002	Tex inducted into Pac-10 Basketball Hall of Honor.
Spring 2003	Coach of the Century—Kansas State University.
	Tex inducted into the University of Southern California Hall of Fame.
Spring 2004	Tex announces his retirement after the All-Star break in February. Phil Jackson retires from coaching at the end of the season.
Fall 2005	Phil Jackson rejoins Los Angeles Lakers as head coach. Tex joins him as assistant coach and consultant.

Lifetime Statistics

Season	Location	Season Results		Location Total		Cumulative Overall Total	
		Win	Lose	Win	Lose	Win	Lose
1947-48	KSU-Assistant	22	6				
1948-49		13	11				
1949-50		17	7				
1950-51		25	4	77	28	77	28
1951-52	Marquette University	9	14				
1952-53		13	11	22	25	99	53
1953-54	KSU-Head Coach	11	10				
1954-55		11	10				
1955-56		17	8				
1956-57		5	8				
1957-58		22	5				
1958-59		25	2				
1959-60		16	10				
1960-61		23	4				
1961-62		22	3				
1962-63		16	9				
1963-64		22	7				
1964-65		12	13				
1965-66		14	11				
1966-67		17	8				
1967-68		19	9	262	117	361	170
1968-69	Univ of Washington	13	13				
1969-70		17	9				
1970-71		15	13	45	35	406	205
1971-72	Houston Rockets	34	38				
1972-73		33	49	67	97	473	302
1973-74	Northwestern University	9	15				
1974-75		6	20				
1975-76		12	15				
1976-77		9	18				
1977-78		8	19	44	87	517	389
1978-79	Long Beach State	16	12				
1979-80		22	12				
1980-81		15	13				
1981-82		12	16				
1982-83		13	16	78	69	595	458
1983-84	Louisiana State Univ	18	11				
1984-85		19	10	37	21	632	479
1985-86	NBA-Chicago Bulls	30	52				
1986-87		40	42				
1987-88		50	32				
1988-89		47	35				
1989-90		55	27				
1990-91		61	21				
1991-92		67	15				
1992-93		57	25				
1993-94		55	27				
1994-95		47	35				
1995-96		72	10				
1996-97		69	13				
1997-98		62	20				
1998-99		13	37				
1999-00		17	65	742	456	1374	935
2000-01	NBA-Los Angeles Lakers	56	26				
2001-02		58	24				
2002-03		50	32				
2003-04		56	26				
2004-05		0	0				
2005-06		45	37	265	145	1639	1080

2719 TOTAL GAMES

60.28% WIN RECORD

Selected Bibliography

Books

Bender, Mark. *Trial by Basketball*. Lenexa, Kansas: Addax Publishing Group, Inc., 2000.

Halberstam, David. *Playing for Keeps*. New York: Random House-Broadway Books, 2000.

Jackson, Phil and Charley Rosen. *More Than a Game*. New York: Seven Stories Press, 2001.

Jackson, Phil with Michael Arkush. *The Last Season: A Team in Search of its Soul*. New York: The Penguin Group, 2004.

Jordan, Michael. *Driven from Within*. Edited by Mark Vancil. New York: Simon & Schuster, Inc.-Atria Books, 2005.

Lazenby, Roland. *Blood on the Horns: The Long Strange Ride of Michael Jordan's Chicago Bulls*. Lenexa, Kansas: Addax Publishing Group, Inc., 1998.

Smith, Sam. *The Jordan Rules*. New York: Simon & Schuster, Inc.-Pocket Books, 1994.

Winter, Fred "Tex." *Triple Post Offense*. New York; Prentice-Hall, 1963.

Numerous *Sports Illustrated* Articles

Newspapers

Chicago Sun Times: Chicago, Illinois

Chicago Tribune: Chicago, Illinois

Kansas City Star: Kansas City, Missouri

Los Angeles Times: Los Angeles, California

Salina Journal: Salina, Kansas

Topeka Capital-Journal: Topeka, Kansas

Wichita Eagle: Wichita, Kansas

Personal Interviews with the Author

Tex Winter

Nancy Winter

Russ Winter

Chris Winter

Brian Winter

Elizabeth Winter Abbott Green

Wynnelle Abbott Turner

Larry Green

Phil Jackson

Kobe Bryant

Frank Hamblen

Pete Newell

Dale Brown

Ernie and Bonnie Barrett

Ken and Dorothy Mahoney

Suggested Further Reading List

Brown, Dale. *Basketball Coaches Organizational Handbook (Art and Science of Coaching)*. Monterey, CA: Coaches Choice Books, 2002.

Christopher, Matt. *On the Court with Kobe Bryant*. New York: Little, Brown and Company, 2001.

Christopher, Matt. *On the Court with Michael Jordan*. New York: Little, Brown and Company, 1996.

Christopher, Matt. *On the Court with Shaquille O'Neal*. New York: Little, Brown and Company, 2005.

Clark, Michael. *Optimum Performance Training: Basketball*. New York: Regan Books, 2006.

Elz, Barry. *Bulls: Portrait of an Era*. Chicago, IL: Tango Publishing International, Inc., 1998.

Garner, Trish, Rob Reheuser, and Zach Bodendieck. *Official NBA Register 2005-06: Every Player, Every Stat*. Saint Louis, MO: Sporting News Publishing, 2005.

Graham, Duey. *OttoMatic: Otto Graham*. Wayne, Michigan: Immortal Investments Publishing, 2004.

Iooss, Walter, and Mark Jacobson. *Hoops: Four Decades of the Pro Game*. New York: Harry N. Abrams, Inc., 2005.

Jackson, Phil. *Sacred Hoops: Spiritual Lessons of a Hardwood Warrior*. New York: Hyperion, 1996.

Krause, Jerry, ed. *Coaching Basketball*. New York: McGraw-Hill, 2002.

Lazenby, Roland. *Mad Game: The NBA Education of Kobe Bryant*. New York: McGraw-Hill, 2002.

Lazenby, Roland. *The Show: The Inside Story of the Spectacular Los Angeles Lakers in the Words of Those Who Lived It*. New York: McGraw-Hill, 2005. (Foreword by Tex Winter)

Leahy, Michael. *When Nothing Else Matters: Michael Jordan's Last Comeback*. New York: Simon & Schuster, 2004.

NBA. *The Perfect Team: The Best Players, Coach, and GM—Let the Debate Begin*. New York: Doubleday Publishing Company, 2006.

Pluto, Terry. *Tall Tales: The Glory Years of the NBA*. Lincoln, NE: University of Nebraska Press, 2000.

Robinson, Rachel. *Jackie Robinson: An Intimate Portrait*. New York: Harry N. Abrams, Inc., 1996.

Smale, David. *The Purple Pinnacle*. Shawnee Mission, KS: Rainbow Publishing, 2002.

Smith, Dean. *Chuck Taylor, All Star: The True Story of the Man Behind the Most Famous Athletic Shoe in History*. Bloomington, IN: Indiana University Press, 2006.

Thompson, Keith R. *Heroes of the Hardcourt: Ranking Pro Basketball's 100 Greatest Players, and Introducing a Whole New Way of Looking at the Game*. Bloomington, IN: Authorhouse, 2005.

Vancil, Mark. *For the Love of the Game: My Story (Michael Jordan)*. New York: Random House-Crown Publishing Group, 1998.

Williams, Pat. *How to Be Like Mike: Life Lessons*. Deerfield Beach, FL: Health Communications, Inc., 2001.

INDEX